The Complete Guide to Baby Naming Ceremonies

Visit our How To website at www.howto.co.uk

At **www.howto.co.uk** you can engage in conversation with our authors – all of whom have 'been there and done that' in their specialist fields. You can get access to special offers and additional content but most importantly you will be able to engage with, and become a part of, a wide and growing community of people just like yourself.

At **www.howto.co.uk** you'll be able to talk and share tips with people who have similar interests and are facing similar challenges in their lives. People who, just like you, have the desire to change their lives for the better – be it through moving to a new country, starting a new business, growing their own vegetables, or writing a novel.

At **www.howto.co.uk** you'll find the support and encouragement you need to help make your aspirations a reality.

You can go direct to
www.complete-guide-to-baby-naming-ceremonies.co.uk
which is part of the main How To site.

How To Books strives to present authentic, inspiring, practical information in their books. Now, when you buy a title from **How To Books**, you get even more than just words on a page.

The
Complete Guide to
Baby Naming
Ceremonies

Becky
Alexander

howtobooks

Permissions

Page 160. 'Us Two' taken from *Now We Are Six* by AA Milne.
Text copyright © The Trustees of the Pooh Properties 1927.
Published by Egmont UK Ltd London and used with permission

Published by How To Books Ltd,
Spring Hill House, Spring Hill Road,
Begbroke, Oxford OX5 1RX
Tel: (01865) 375794. Fax: (01865) 379162
info@howtobooks.co.uk
www.howtobooks.co.uk

Every effort has been made to identify and acknowledge the sources of the
material quoted throughout this book. The author and publishers apologise for
any errors or omissions, and would be grateful to be notified of any corrections
that should appear in any reprint or new edition.

How To Books greatly reduce the carbon footprint of their books by sourcing
their typesetting and printing in the UK.

British Library Catalog
A catalogue record fo

ISBN: 978-1-84528-41

Produced for How To
Cover and text design
Printed and bound by

NOTE: The material co
guidance and no liabil
result of relying in part
The laws and regulatio

check the current posit... .... .c.cvant authorities before making personal
arrangements.

Contents

⟶⟶ CHAPTER 3 ⟵⟵

∾ **CHAPTER 4** ⬿

~~ CHAPTER 5 ~~

~~ CHAPTER 6 ~~

CHAPTER ONE

Introduction

A New Trend

The arrival of a new baby or child into your lives is one of the most exciting events in a family's life, and many of us want to celebrate the occasion in a special, memorable way. Up until fairly recently, the only way to celebrate this rite of passage was in your local place of worship, and there wasn't much alternative. But since the growing popularity of civil weddings, people have started to think about something similar for babies and children. Now you can have a civil naming ceremony at your local registry office, or in a venue of your choice, and almost anything goes!

As this is quite a new trend in the UK, this book collects together in one place everything you might need to plan your own naming ceremony. It is full of poems, readings, ideas for things to say and special ways to mark the day. There is no legal requirement in a naming ceremony, so you can choose the words and readings that suit you and your family. Your naming ceremony can be relaxed or formal, simple or involving lots of family, you can hold it indoors or outdoors … you can make it unique to your family and to each child.

Many families would like to celebrate the arrival of a new child in some way but feel that the traditional religious ceremony just isn't for them. So in the absence of an alternative this amazing occasion has gone by quietly. Many of the people I interviewed in researching this book have wanted to bring their closest friends and family together to celebrate but they just weren't sure how to do so. In our busy lives it is not always easy to get all your favourite people together in one place, and we need to seize all the chances we get! Your family and friends get the chance to meet the new arrival, and catch up with old faces. Your new child gets to know very early on in his or her life that he or she is part of a wider community, who love and care for them.

The parents I interviewed wanted something simple but meaningful. They wanted to welcome the child into their family and this was particularly the case when the child has older siblings. Older children really love naming ceremonies, especially if they have a role to play. And almost everyone interviewed said that wanted to have a few glasses of something fizzy to celebrate!

It is worth knowing that even religious ceremonies have often been held in the home – there is no formal need to hold them in a place of worship. Home christenings have always taken place. Some of the traditions we associate with christenings come from a range of backgrounds, some Christian, some pagan. So if you choose to include a particular element, such as lighting a candle in your ceremony, then you are absolutely entitled to do so.

Naming ceremonies have been around for years now. One friend told me that she held naming ceremonies for her sons in California almost 20 years ago, guided by a Shaman. The Humanist Society have been offering a simple naming ceremony that families can hold in their own home for a number of years – an experienced celebrant can lead the ceremony for you and help you plan readings and poems.

The celebrity magazines have been publishing glossy photos of naming ceremonies held by celebrities for some years but it is only in the past year that it has been possible to hold a naming ceremony at a local register office. Lord Michael Young established the Baby Naming Society in 1994 and was instrumental to the introduction of baby naming ceremonies in 1998 by the then Home Secretary Jack Straw. As a result, you can now contact your local register office and they can advise you on how to hold a ceremony and provide an experienced celebrant. This book can help you to plan a naming ceremony, whether you envisage using the register office service or devising something unique to you.

A new choice for parents

Naming ceremonies are still fairly new to the UK so you might need to explain to friends and family how it is going to work. This is especially important if you feel that some may have been expecting a christening. It is a really good idea to include a brief outline of the event when you send out invitations so they know what to expect. There is no need to go into detailed explanations or running orders. Outline the venue and timing of the event and indicate whether food will be provided.

You might like to add that poems and readings will be said, followed by any details of a special event. For example, if you plan to plant a tree in your garden you could add a note saying 'bring your wellies'. Letting guests know what is going to happen will help to avoid well-meaning comments on the day about what is happening next and comparisons to traditional ceremonies.

Some guests may not agree with your choice, preferring a traditional religious ceremony. One way to help with this is to ask them to read a prayer if you feel that would be comfortable for you. But at the end of the day it is your choice and, as naming ceremonies become more popular, they will become familiar to your friends and family.

What is a naming ceremony?

You are required by law to register the birth of a child at your local register office. This is a short, simple task where, having made an appointment, you complete the birth certificate with the help of the registrar and sign the birth register so the government knows that this new person exists.

A naming ceremony is not a legal requirement (unlike a civil marriage) so you don't have to do it at a register office. You could, however, follow your trip to the register office with a party or ceremony at home. You do have to register the birth of your child within 42 days of his or her birth, so this often means that many parents do not have the time or energy to plan a big family gathering for the same day. It is also very usual for the mother to register the child while in hospital, so the event can come and go before you are ready to organise a naming ceremony.

Parents now have the option to hold a naming ceremony for their child at a register office. This is a non-religious ceremony that celebrates the birth of a child. You can also hold one to welcome new children into the family, such as adopted children. The parents can nominate adults to support their child, which is a bit like nominating a godfather and godmother at a christening. You need to show the birth certificate when you make the ceremony booking. At the end of the register office ceremony you are given a certificate, but this is not a legal document and you don't need to have one – it simply marks the occasion.

You can hold a meaningful and special naming ceremony in your own home, garden or in fact at any venue of your choice.

A naming ceremony is simply a way of getting friends and family together to celebrate the arrival of a new child. You can give the event a sense of ritual and ceremony by including special words, reading poems and asking family and friends to contribute in some way. It's an opportunity to stand up in front of your favourite people and tell them that you plan to be the very best parents you can and to ask them to help you in achieving this goal.

A new choice for parents

I asked some parents why they chose a naming ceremony and here are some of their responses:

- 'We don't go to church so it felt wrong to have a christening, but we still wanted to do something.'
- 'My sister held a naming ceremony for her first baby and we all loved it. It was a fantastic day when everyone got together and we wanted to do something similar. She read a poem at our daughter's naming ceremony and it felt as if a tradition was being passed on.'
- 'We wanted to have a party to get everyone together to celebrate the arrival of Charlie. We held it on his first birthday and it was a really special day.'
- 'We had a civil wedding and we wanted to do something similar when Grace arrived. The hall we got married in also does naming ceremonies so it felt like the right place.'
- 'We didn't do anything for our first daughter, and we felt we missed out when other people were talking about christenings and we wanted to do something. So when we heard about naming ceremonies, we did one for our second child.'

> 🖐 'We have friends who we would like to be godparents but they are not religious and a naming ceremony seemed like the way to involve the people who are important to us. We still read some prayers at the ceremony and it worked for us.'
>
> 🖐 'We didn't have a wedding and this was our opportunity to get everyone together.'

Welcome your child to the world

Birthdays, weddings and funerals are important rites of passage and we need them to mark the key moments in our lives. The arrival of a new baby is a fantastic thing and yet many people don't mark the occasion in a special way. Even when you are sleep-deprived and wondering how life is ever going to get back to normal, it makes sense to bring family and friends together to celebrate this new person. A naming ceremony can be a wonderful way to bring everyone together, and it gives family and friends an opportunity to congratulate you and offer support.

There is no specific date that you have to hold a ceremony on – you can wait until the new mum has recovered from the birth and everyone has settled into family life. When you are ready, a naming ceremony is a wonderful opportunity to introduce your new child to your closest friends and family, and to bring them together on one day. Parents, siblings and special adults can promise in front of others to care for the child, further strengthening family and friendship bonds. And of course, it is a great opportunity to have a fantastic party!

What are your options?

Do it yourself

One of the best ways to hold a naming ceremony is to plan it yourselves. Choose a venue (home is just fine) and pick a date that everyone important to you can make. Sit down with your partner and plan what you would like to happen. You will find plenty of ideas in this book for readings, things to say, promises, music choices and fun ways to make the event special. You can welcome guests just as you would to, say, a birthday party.

When everyone is gathered, you can take it in turns to lead the ceremony or one of you can look after the child while the other says any words that you wish to. If your child is quite young, keep the ceremony short so he or she doesn't get too tired. You may find it more relaxing and enjoyable if you involve a friend or celebrant. It completely depends on how relaxed or formal you want the ceremony to be, and if your guests are happy to wait or get involved if needed. You may also just feel too emotional on the day and prefer someone else to be responsible for saying the words you have planned – you could always have this as a back-up plan if you think this is likely to be you!

If you decide to organise the ceremony yourselves, make time beforehand to write down everything that you might need help with. This could be, for example, help with the food and drinks, help looking after siblings, someone to take photographs or make a DVD of the key moments, and someone to welcome latecomers. Make sure that anyone who is kind enough to help also gets to be there at the key moments and does not miss any part of the ceremony.

Ask a friend to help

If you have a confident friend or family member who has held their own naming ceremony, you could ask him or her to lead the ceremony for you. You could meet with your chosen person beforehand to go through what you would like to happen. Preparing a typed outline of who is going to say what and the words of any poems would be helpful so that they do not have to spend too long preparing for it.

A humanist ceremony

Humanism is non-religious and is based on the wish that people should make the most of life and try to help others to do so also. In their own words, 'humanism is an approach to life based on reason and our common humanity, recognizing that moral values are properly founded on human nature and experience alone'.

The British Humanist Association is a charity that can provide non-religious naming ceremonies, as well as weddings and funerals. They can lead a naming ceremony for you and can make it unique to your family. They do not give you a set order of ceremony to follow, but can give you some ideas and can provide an experienced celebrant to lead the ceremony. You meet with the celebrant beforehand to decide on what you wish to say and which readings you want.

The ceremony can follow any structure you like but they tend to start with a welcome to all the guests, with the celebrant saying a few words of welcome along with something about the parents and why they have chosen this ceremony. This is followed by a naming part, in which the parents hold the child so that everyone in the room can see and they or the celebrant announce the name and the reasons for this chosen name. The parents may then say promises to the child, followed by the words or promises from the supporting adults, if you are having any. You can also include siblings and other members of the family.

A civil naming ceremony

A civil naming ceremony is the civil equivalent of a christening. Unlike a civil wedding, there is no legal requirement and you can choose almost any words and readings you like. You can hold a civil naming in your local register office, home, or at a venue such as a hotel or village hall and a registrar will lead the ceremony for you.

You meet with the registrar beforehand to go through the content of the ceremony. This can be a great way forward, especially if this is your first child and you like the idea of an experienced person leading the event. To book a registrar, simply contact your local register office. There will be a cost, depending on the time, day and venue of the ceremony. See page 85 for the phrases and words used during a register office naming ceremony.

The registrar will confirm the child's name and the parents declare promises to their child, such as to love him or her and to provide a caring and loving home. Other key people, such as grandparents, friends and siblings, can say a few words or read a poem. You can include poems and readings that are special to you. You can also include music at the beginning or end.

If you pick up a guide to ceremonies from your local register office you will find adverts for places that host civil weddings and many are now also experienced at hosting naming ceremonies. The benefit of this is that you can hold a party in the venue afterwards, with them doing the catering.

Freelance celebrants

There are several organisations and individuals that can provide an experienced celebrant who can organise and lead a naming ceremony for you. Civil Naming Ceremonies (see page 178) is one of the most experienced, but you can also find individual celebrants who may share your values and beliefs more closely and can make a ceremony personal to you.

What to call your ceremony?

One of the first things you will find out when you start to plan a naming ceremony is that people may have a different name for what you are doing, such as a civil naming, a blessing or a thanksgiving. If you don't plan to hold the ceremony in a religious or registry building, then you can call your ceremony anything you like. If your parents, for example, would feel more comfortable with it being called a 'blessing' then you might want to do that, even if you plan to hold the ceremony in your back garden. If you want to call it a 'welcome' party, a 'naming day', or a 'celebration', then go ahead.

Some of these terms have specific meaning in the Christian church. It is useful to know this so that you don't choose something that really doesn't work for you.

🖐 Blessing: Associated with the Baptist Christian church whereby parents, family and the church community give thanks for the arrival of the baby. They do not make religious promises on his or her behalf, leaving that until the child or adult wishes to make that decision for him or herself.

- Christening: A traditional baby naming ceremony held in church to welcome the child to the congregation. Parents and godparents promise to raise the child in the Christian church and with Christian values.
- Thanksgiving: This is an option held in most Christian places of worship, where thanks are given for the birth of a child. Parents may make promises, and this is a good option if you want to include key adults in the ceremony but they are not religious themselves.

What if you want to include religion?

It does happen that parents want some element of religious tradition in their ceremony, either because the grandparents may have wanted a christening or because one parent may have faith but does not belong to a local church. If this is the case, you could consider one person reading a prayer or extract from the Bible during the ceremony; there is certainly no reason why you cannot and it may offer a great way to include all views in the family. If you are planning to invite a humanist celebrant to lead the ceremony, then this probably won't work for them but do talk it through first.

You may also decide to have a large family gathering that is non-religious, with poems and readings, and then have a small, private blessing at a place of worship. Choose whatever makes you feel comfortable.

Making everyone feel welcome

Naming ceremonies are, of course, family events. There will probably be a range of ages from grandparents to very young children, so bear this in mind with your planning. If you have young children there, you will need to keep the ceremony short and flexible. If you have friends doing readings, then they need to be warned that there will be lots of children and that you will be very understanding if they have to pause mid-stream! You may want to keep it short, or break up the ceremony into small parts.

- Make sure there is space for children to move about, or that they have time to run around and play before the ceremony starts. Provide some entertainment or some toys to keep them busy and happy. You might want to have some snacks on hand that parents can help themselves to for the children.

- If you know guests have had a long journey make sure there are drinks and simple snacks on offer at arrival, whether you go for tea and cakes or champagne and nibbles. It can help to refresh everyone and lift spirits after a journey.

- If you have lots of older members of the family present, make sure there is the option for sitting down at some point in the party.

- If you have guests from different faiths or nationalities, you may like to include them by asking them to read a prayer or a blessing that is special to them. All cultures celebrate the arrival of a child in some way, so it is a wonderful opportunity to bring together loved ones with different backgrounds and to let them bring their own experiences to the occasion.

Welcoming a stepchild or adopted child

There is absolutely no reason why you cannot hold a naming ceremony for a new stepchild or adopted child. It would be a lovely way to celebrate their arrival into your family with extended family and friends. Of course with a stepchild there is no need to announce a name, but you may like to choose a simple ceremony that welcomes him or her to the family. It could be an opportunity to announce a new surname. You may prefer to call it a 'welcome party'. You could ask siblings to read a poem and choose one of the special ways to mark the day (see Chapter 4).

With an adopted child, you could still hold a naming ceremony and introduce him or her to the family. It would be a very valuable way of letting everyone know that the much longed for child has now arrived, and you want to celebrate the fact. You can tell everyone that you are excited about your child's arrival, and make the same promises to love and care for the child as you would with a baby.

Ceremonies around the world

Goddess naming ceremony

A goddess naming ceremony begins with a welcome to all by the priestess and a brief description of the ceremony to follow. The goddess priestess calls to the deities of the five directions, which include the elements of air, fire, water and earth. Family, friends and special adults (sponsors) are included in each stage. Each element is symbolised during the ceremony. For example, when the goddess calls to the power of air, guests or the child can blow fairy bubbles or be given feathers. When she calls to fire, she can light a candle. Earth can be symbolised by giving earth to the child to hold or by sprinkling a mixture of glitter and soil. The child may also be given a crystal or stone. Poetry, music and readings can also be included. For more information on goddess ceremonies, see Further Reading (page 178).

Hindu naming ceremony

Naming a baby is considered sacred and is an important Indian tradition. Known as Namkaran or Namakaran Sanskar, a Hindu naming ceremony can be an elaborate occasion. It is usually held ten days after a baby's delivery. The house is cleaned and sanctified for the ceremony. The mother and child are bathed traditionally, dressed in new clothes and the mother wets the head of the baby with water as a symbol of purifying the child. The baby is then handed over to the paternal grandmother or the father who sits near the priest during the ritual. The sacred fire is lit and the priest chants sacred hymns to invoke the gods in the heaven to bless the child.

According to the date and time of the child's birth, a particular letter of the Sanskrit alphabet is chosen and the baby is then given a name starting with that letter. Usually the father whispers the name four times in the right ear of the baby. The baby receives blessings from all, including the priests. A feast is organised for the priests and the guests to celebrate the occasion.

Buddhist naming ceremony

Buddhist communities generally do not mark or celebrate events in a lifecycle, as the belief is that beings go through a succession of lifetimes. But parents may choose to hold a very simple naming ceremony in which the child's name is announced to the community. The Buddhist monk leader takes the selected name, which often has a meaning, and blesses the baby with this meaning and name. The family is able to invite close friends. The emphasis is on the idea that they celebrate a rebirth of a soul into a new human form.

Jewish naming ceremony

In Judaism, baby girls have a Zeved Habat ceremony usually within the first month following birth. It may be celebrated privately in the synagogue or in a party at home. The mother will say a thanksgiving and the friends and family will recite the Song of Songs and a name-giving prayer. The ceremony will usually be lead by a rabbi.

Many Jewish boys are circumcised and named on the eighth day after birth during a Brit Milah ceremony. A Brit Shalom naming ceremony is an option, whereby the parents choose for the child not to be circumcised and instead include a symbolic act.

Sikh naming ceremony

Known as a Naam Karan, a Sikh naming ceremony usually takes place as soon as the mother and child are fit enough to attend the Gurdwara. There is no rush, and parents can take time to organise the occasion and invite friends and family.

Karah prasad is eaten to celebrate the occasion. It is a type of halva made with equal portions of semolina, butter and sugar to symbolise equality amongst men and women. Everyone at the ceremony will eat a piece.

Prayers and readings are said to request good health for the child and to ask for the name of the child. The first letter of the first word of the hukam (a random piece of Sikh scripture) is the letter to be used to give the name to the child (this is arranged before the ceremony). Once the name for the baby has been chosen, 'Kaur' is added to the names of girls and 'Singh' is added to the names of boys.

Japanese naming day

The Japanese tradition is to hold a naming ceremony on the seventh day after a child is born. Each year Japan holds a children's day when the entire country celebrates children with special food and games.

Wicca naming ceremony

At an initiation or dedication ritual, the baby or child takes a Wiccan name, which is not used in public but only among other Wiccans in religious gatherings. For adult Wiccans, taking a Wiccan name symbolises a rebirth.

The question of godparents

One of the reasons people choose to have a naming ceremony is that they want to include special adults in their child's life and to mark this in some way. Even if the parents are religious often their closest friends are not, and this can lead to the decision not to hold a christening.

The term 'godparent' has specific meaning to the Christian church and so is not really suitable if you or the person you choose is not religious. Other words you can choose include 'sponsor', 'supporting adult', or you may go down the more relaxed route and use 'fairy godmother'! In some ways it probably doesn't matter, as you don't need to declare it at a ceremony – the key thing is that your child knows what to call them as they grow up.

One modern solution is to use the adults who you cite in your will to look after your child in the event of you being unable to do so. In legal terms, these adults are called 'guardians' and a naming ceremony could be a very useful way to make this known to your wider circle. For example, if you choose your brother and his partner to be guardians, then they can be named during the naming ceremony and they might contribute a poem or reading. There is no need to spell out what a guardian means and so bring a negative note to the party – you are simply involving them in a special way.

Whatever you choose to call the special adults, you decide what role you want them to play. You may want them to make promises to you and the child at the ceremony, and you can go through the words together before the event. If they have never done it before, make time to explain what the ceremony means to you and how it will work on the day. Most people will be delighted to be asked and may be relieved that they are not expected to make a religious commitment. You may simply want them to be there on the day and to read a poem or help in some way, such as hold the child. Just knowing that they are there for you may be enough, without the need for special words.

As you are not holding the naming ceremony in a church, there is no limit on how many or how few guardians you choose. You may say that the whole group of guests gathered there that day are guardians, or you may choose just one person who is special to you and your partner.

CHAPTER TWO

Planning the event

When to hold the naming ceremony

It is entirely up to you when you choose to hold the naming ceremony. There is a legal requirement that you register the name of the child within 42 days of the birth, but you don't have to hold your naming ceremony on the same day, unless you would like to combine the two.

It really depends on how much energy you as new parents have and when you think you will be ready to enjoy the naming ceremony. Many first-time parents find the first few months with a new baby quite tiring and have enough to get used to without organising a party. However, you may feel it is important to hold the ceremony as soon as possible after the birth to formally introduce the baby to your wider circle of family and friends. As long as you ask for a little help with the planning or the catering, then you should be able to enjoy it too.

Between four and six months is a popular time to hold the ceremony as the child is more likely to be in a reasonable sleeping pattern, and the parents may be more able to work out when he or she will be awake and able to enjoy lots of attention. You may like to hold the naming ceremony on your wedding anniversary, especially if you plan to go back to the same venue.

On your child's first birthday

One of the most popular dates for holding a naming ceremony is on a child's first birthday. You can combine the event with a birthday party, which helps to keep it relaxed and informal and can mean that guests are more familiar with what may happen on the day. As your child may well be crawling or even running around you will need to carefully consider your choice of venue, as space to explore will make life easier for everyone. You may choose to have entertainment for children and this can give the parents a chance to relax and catch up with guests.

Before naming ceremonies became widespread, people often used the first birthday as the first opportunity to bring friends and family together to celebrate the arrival of a new child. If you felt that a christening was not for you, then a first birthday can be a good focus for celebration. If you have family and friends that live far from you it can make sense to combine both occasions, and if you are the first in your group of friends or family to have a naming ceremony it can be a good way to introduce the naming ceremony elements to them. See page 73 for ideas for what to say.

You can combine a whole naming ceremony with the birthday party or just certain elements. You may decide that you want to include some more formal elements, such as a welcome speech, which would not usually happen at a birthday party. You could also include poems read by older siblings or mark the day in some way, such as by planting a tree, sponsoring a child or gathering a book of wishes. If you tell people what you plan to do, either in the invitations or in your welcome speech, they will know what to expect and this can help the event to run smoothly.

If you plan to include a whole ceremony then do it at the start of the party. Keep the ceremony fairly short, so there is time for the children to play afterwards. You may like to provide large toys to play with, be outside in a garden or arrange entertainment.

A naming ceremony for older children

If your children are older, if you have more than one child and wish them to have a shared naming day, or if you have adopted children, then you can still hold a naming ceremony for them. You can adjust the ceremony to include the children in a more active way: they might read a simple poem or something they have written themselves, or they could plant a tree or sprinkle seeds. Many religions have ceremonies for older children (for example, confirmation) so it is not as unusual as it may first seem.

Combining a naming ceremony and wedding

In many ways it makes perfect sense to combine a wedding with a naming ceremony. You can discuss it with the registrar or celebrant beforehand and they can perform the naming ceremony after the wedding. It can be an opportunity to make promises to each other, and to your children, and you can go forward into the future as a family. Your family and friends are all gathered together which might not happen on another occasion. It also makes sense to combine both ceremonies if you are using a special location and catering.

As a wedding is a legal ceremony, it is possible that you may have a different registrar for each ceremony depending on its location and timing. If you prefer you could hold the wedding and then later in the day do the naming ceremony, even perhaps conducting it yourselves or with help from an independent celebrant or friend.

When you invite people to the wedding and naming ceremony, make it clear on the invitations that you plan to include both events and what guests should expect in terms of timing. Provide an order of service when people arrive. This can indicate if you plan to hold the naming ceremony in another part of the home or venue, such as the garden. This can help to prevent people missing any part of the ceremony, thinking that it has finished. You could say that there will be a short break between ceremonies if this would help those with young children. Giving a rough timing of the event will also help special adults involved in the ceremony, as they know when they will be needed to join in. See page 73 for ideas on what to say.

You can ask your celebrant to include a few words or promises for you to make to your child. You can simply include one or two more vows at the end of your service. For example, you could ask a special friend or family member to hold your child and then pass him or her to you. Both parents can then say together, 'We promise to love and care for [child's name] together'. You could make it more formal and include more vows and a reading or poem, and also ask your special friends and family to join you at the front with the celebrant.

One lovely idea is to have a tiered wedding cake, with one section iced for the naming ceremony. This could be the smallest layer and it could be decorated in a slightly different way. Perhaps it could be a sponge cake rather than traditional fruit so that it is more child-friendly. Cupcakes decorated with different coloured rosebuds also works well – each colour could represent one person in the family.

Choosing a time for the ceremony

You can choose to hold a ceremony at any time of the day; here are some tips to consider:

- When will your child be at his or her most awake and happy? If it is in the morning, plan around that. Try to avoid holding the ceremony at a key nap time, as it could be too much for your child. Factor in that meeting lots of new people will be extra-stimulating and exciting.
- Do your guests have far to travel? If many of them have more than an hour to travel, it may be best to hold the ceremony in the afternoon so they can arrive relaxed.
- Does your chosen venue have restrictions on when naming ceremonies can take place? Wedding ceremonies tend to happen near midday or early afternoon to allow time for wedding receptions, so you may find your choice is limited to mornings at certain venues.
- If you are using a professional celebrant, find out his or her availability. They can usually do any time, but it depends on bookings. In the summer you may find that they are very booked up with weddings, so you may need to book ahead, particularly at register offices.
- What kind of food and drinks would you like to serve? If you would like to serve sparkling wine, then the afternoon might be best. If your ceremony will finish at a meal time then you will need to factor that in to your planning, as people may expect a meal and children will certainly need to eat something.

Brunch party theme

A morning ceremony can be an excellent option for those with a baby or young children as they are often at their best at this time. Venues are often more available and traditional christenings tend to be held in the morning. The key is to keep the ceremony simple so you don't have too much to do first thing. Food can be light, yet delicious, and people won't expect a full meal, which can make life easier. Bear in mind how far your family and friends will have to travel and if it might be difficult for them to get to you by mid-morning; an afternoon ceremony might be easier.

 **Time and place**

A morning brunch is one of the most relaxed ways to host a naming ceremony and it would be an ideal option for holding at home or in your garden. 11 am makes an ideal start time, giving everyone time to get ready. You could welcome your guests with a light brunch first, and then follow with the ceremony when everyone is relaxed and refreshed. Two hours is probably more than enough for a baby or young child to enjoy, so keep it fairly short. It is a good idea to include the start and end times on the invitation so people know what is going to happen and what food will be provided.

Aim for a relaxed feel in the room. There is no need for formal tableware – provide piles of napkins and jugs of juice, and encourage people to help themselves. You could place jam jars of flowers around the room. Keep any music you choose light to suit the atmosphere of the morning.

 **Food**

Brunch is such an easy option, yet one that many guests will enjoy. Plates piled high with filled bagels and warmed croissants or blueberry muffins are very easy to prepare. There is no need to use plates; just make sure there are plenty of thick napkins to hand around.

Fill toasted bagels with crispy bacon and egg mayonnaise, mozzarella and tomato, or smoked salmon and cream cheese. If you have time, or a willing friend, hot bacon sandwiches would be very popular.

Have plates of fruits around the room for children and adults to snack on, such as strawberries and melon wedges in the summer, and ripe plums in the autumn. You can add one or two pots of jam.

 Drinks

As it is morning, guests will probably appreciate coffee and tea or fruit juice when they arrive, so it would be a good idea to provide this. If you plan to do the catering yourself, you could look into borrowing or hiring hot water urns or very large flasks that hold freshly prepared coffee or tea. Put out lots of cups, more than you think you need, and put up a sign asking everyone to help themselves to refills.

Once people are settled in, you can offer champagne or sparkling wine, perhaps mixed with freshly squeezed orange juice for buck's fizz, or elderflower cordial for an English twist.

 Ideas for poems

♪ 'Through baby's eyes' – author unknown (see page 130)
♪ 'Now this is the day' – Zuni Indians (see page 133)
♪ 'Lottie' – Lucy Payne (see page 142)

---

tips

'All Things Bright and Beautiful'

If you would like your guests to sing together, 'All Things Bright and Beautiful' makes a great choice as most people will know it – and it does feel appropriate for singing in the morning. If you have older children, they may like to sing it for others to listen to!

---

tips

Keep it short and simple

The key to a relaxed and happy naming ceremony is to keep it short and simple. As babies and young children will be present, you will only have a short time to keep everyone's attention and it is sensible to go with that rather than hoping that everyone will sit quietly for more than half an hour. Keep things a little flexible too – for example, you may have a more formal part to the ceremony, with a break before poems and readings.

A welcome and promises will take about ten minutes. Involving more people and more readings can make a ceremony last for half an hour, and this would be a sensible maximum. If you would like to include more elements, such as planting a tree for which you need to move outside, include a break for people to attend to young children or make trips to the loo.

Allow plenty of time for food, drinks and socialising afterwards – at least an hour. This will allow time for the parents to catch up with family and friends and for photographs to be taken. Children can run around and let off steam.

What to wear

For baby

Traditional christening clothes tend to be white or cream and fairly formal. If you have an heirloom gown in the family there is no reason why you cannot use it for a naming ceremony. A gown can actually be a practical choice for nappy changing, although the delicate fabrics often used are not always easy to keep clean.

If you prefer, any outfit that your baby feels comfortable in will be ideal. You could dress him or her in a nice babygro, and simply wrap him or her in a pretty blanket or shawl for warmth and protection. A dress or smart trousers and top would also be good. If you find something special and expensive, you could keep it for another child in the family or sell it online to recoup some of the cost.

Whatever you choose for your baby make sure that you can change his or her nappy easily, in case of last minute emergencies. Also have a good change of clothes with you, or give them to a friend to look after, in case of feeding spills. Have a large muslin or nice cloth with you in case of dribbles on baby or on you!

If you kept a wedding dress or bridesmaid outfit you may like to use this to make a gown or shawl for your baby's special outfit.

For you

Whatever you choose to wear, make sure that you feel comfortable in it and can hold your baby with comfort. Jackets with tight sleeves can feel uncomfortable when lifting a baby on to your shoulder.

For siblings

Older siblings may like to wear something special too – perhaps something that matches your outfit or the baby's outfit, such as a matching colour. It can help them to feel included.

Choosing a venue

As there is no legal requirement to a naming ceremony, you can choose any venue you like! There is no need to hold it in a register office, although it can be a very good option. You can hold it at home, in your garden, at a local church hall, on the beach, in the woods, at a favourite café, at a hotel or wedding venue, or at a local zoo or aquarium.

Start by thinking about how many people you want to invite, and remember to include all children and that they will need plenty of space for running around. If you plan to hold a large party then you may find it more enjoyable to book a hotel or wedding venue, which can provide a good-sized room or marquee and organise the drinks and catering for you. Somewhere with a garden would be ideal. You may have recently got married or held a family party in a local venue, and it could be a good choice to hold the naming ceremony there as well.

Some venues will have experience of holding naming ceremonies, but for many it is a new thing. They may be experienced at hosting weddings and birthday parties, so you can draw on that experience. There is no need to be tied to a wedding package or a set meal. A naming ceremony is usually a much simpler occasion and people won't want or expect to sit down to eat three courses. A relaxed buffet, afternoon tea or barbecue would probably work better, especially with young children. Don't be afraid to ask for what you want. You may be booking the ceremony for the morning, which can be a quiet time in a hotel, so they should be able to be more flexible than for a wedding.

If you hold the naming ceremony at the same place as your wedding, you could consider holding it on your wedding anniversary – and if you kept a layer of cake, this is the time to get it out!

A favourite restaurant or café may be a good venue, as long as you can fit everyone in comfortably. If you want the ceremony to be in the morning, they may be very happy to accommodate you if it is usually a quiet time for them. They would expect to be involved in the catering, so plan a meeting well in advance and talk through your ideas. Check that the food they provide is of the standard you usually get when you go in there and tell them anything you particularly like – for example, if you love their lemon cake, let them know so they can provide it.

A church hall in your local community can often be hired out for birthday parties, toddler groups etc., but it might be worth mentioning the reason for your booking when you make arrangements for a naming ceremony just to avoid any awkward moments on the day. Some religious groups may feel uncomfortable with a ceremony of a non-religious kind going on in their premises, so it makes sense to be open and respectful to their wishes too. There are many public venues, from town halls and scout huts to school halls, so you are bound to find something suitable. Anywhere that hosts children's birthday parties may be suitable for a naming ceremony, so if you love your local zoo or park, do ask them.

═checklist ☑═

Venue checklist

☐ Is the room big enough for all your guests? Will they need to sit or stand, and will there be room for chairs for all? Will there be room for people to stand and talk before the ceremony starts?

☐ Can children move around safely and easily?

☐ Where will the celebrant, parents and child be standing? Is there space in a corner, at the front of the room or in an alcove? Will everyone be able to see and hear you?

☐ Is the room appropriate for the time of day you want to be in there? For example, the décor of many hotel function rooms can be quite dark as it is often designed for evening parties. What does it look like in the morning?

☐ Ask if there will be any other events going on that day and will the area be open to the public.

☐ Is there parking for everyone who needs it?

☐ Is the location of the room or marquee easy to find, or are signs or people needed to guide guests?

☐ Are there tables and windowsills for people to balance drinks and plates?

☐ Is there easy access for buggies, prams and wheelchairs, if required? Where can people park buggies if they need to, so that they are out of the way but easily accessible?

☐ Can you or someone else come in early to get the room ready and to decorate it?

☐ Where will people put gifts, cards, coats and bags?

☐ Are there enough loos for your guests? A café may only have one toilet, which could be annoying if you have 40 people arriving at the same time!

Holding the ceremony at home

This can be the best option for many families, as it can be a relaxing, comfortable, and affordable choice. However, you do need to consider if you have space for everyone to move about comfortably and enough chairs for those who need to sit down. Will the streets around your home provide adequate parking for everyone who is coming, or can you arrange for parking at a nearby hall or school?

If you hold it at home decide where the actual ceremony will take place (such as in your main living room) and work out if you need to move furniture beforehand and if you will need help to do this. Give thought to how you are going to serve food and drinks. As the parents you will be busy looking after your child and your guests, being in photos, talking to the celebrant and trying to have a lovely time, so you will definitely need help with this part.

It is a good idea to discuss what help you need with your family and friends beforehand so they can be forewarned. It might be cost-effective to get in outside caterers; this can still be more affordable than eating in a restaurant and you can have more control over what is on the menu. Perhaps some sensible older teenagers in the family can be paid to help, which would also help prevent them from getting bored.

Bear in mind the following points, so you are not surprised by something on the day:

- Where can people park buggies, and put coats and bags? You could ask someone to be in charge of this, and to take coats and bags upstairs for you. Will people with sleeping babies need to bring a buggy inside? Choose a quiet room where they can put a sleeping baby.
- How many people will want to sit down? Can you borrow or hire extra chairs?
- Do you have space for some toys on the floor without people tripping over them?
- Can you move outside for some of the ceremony or party? Are there chairs and tables outside?
- Is there space in the kitchen to get out plenty of plates, glasses, serving dishes etc? Is it helpful to put up another small table to put things on?
- If you have pets, where will they be during the ceremony? Will they be ok with lots of people in your home?

Choosing a colour scheme

Colour has a powerful effect on mood and it can be used to create a certain atmosphere at a naming ceremony. For example, white decorations, flowers and clothes can appear very fresh and spiritual. White is often connected with ceremonial clothes, so can evoke a sense of special occasion. Yellow and orange colour schemes can feel very warm and cheerful. You may be drawn to a colour and use it for your child's naming day simply because you all love it and it makes you feel good.

Many cultures have devised colour systems with religious or secular meaning. These are some of the most popular:

- **Blue:** Associated with the sky and sea. It is spiritual, spacious and associated with hope.
- **Red:** Bright red is the colour of fire and is a symbol of a strong life force. Throughout Asia, red is a lucky colour. Buddhists consider it the colour of activity and creativity. In the West red is the colour of love and beauty.
- **Green:** Associated with nature, fertility, hope, renewal and rebirth. Green is a sacred colour in Islam, representing fertility and spiritual knowledge. In the West it is the colour of spring and represents the start of a new life-cycle.
- **Yellow:** Associated with the sun, youth and energy. Bring in yellow flowers to bring in sunshine and warmth.
- **Purple:** This rich colour is associated with wealth, royalty, nobility and ceremony. In nature lavender, orchids, lilac and violet are considered delicate and precious.
- **White:** This pure colour is actually made up of all the colours in the spectrum. It is associated with ceremonies, stillness, quiet and potential.

Beach party theme

Is there a better British location than a long sandy beach, backed with sand dunes and the occasional beach hut? As the UK is an island, it is only a couple of hours in any direction at most to the nearest beach and a beach would make a lovely relaxing place to hold a chilled-out naming ceremony. Many people feel a spiritual connection to the sea and a beach can be a magical place to get married or hold a naming ceremony.

Choose a spot that is away from the main crowds and, if possible, one that offers some natural protection from breezes. You could put up some pretty windbreaks and flags to create a sense of place and occasion, as well as showing people where you are based. Hang up some bunting and put out some rugs.

You can be as organised or relaxed as you like. You might want to have a back-up plan in case of windy or rainy weather, such as a local café or large beach hut. You could tell guests that you will postpone if the weather is not great; for a small occasion such as a naming ceremony, this is certainly possible. You could even wait until later in the day.

If you have lots of young children with you, get someone to be in charge of beach games and sandcastle building. Bring a bag of buckets and spades and ask them to build a huge sandcastle or sea creature. This might be a good way to keep children entertained while you do the ceremony and readings.

Time and place

Tell everyone where on the beach you plan to meet. You could all walk to the spot together if it is easier, or provide a drawn map. You could stick small flags into the sand en route so guests can find you – but don't rely on them as they might be borrowed by small children along the way! If you can, put up a tent or gazebo so people with small children can rest or shelter if needed, or find shade. It can also be a place for people to leave bags, and store food, drinks and gifts.

Beach hut

You can hire beach huts via many websites by the day or hour, and they can make a great base or location for the naming ceremony. Some are very small and fit only a couple of people inside at a time, but you could arrange chairs, blankets or cushions in front of the hut for guests to sit on. The celebrant, parents and child can stand inside or in front of the beach hut during the ceremony.

Food

Keep it really simple for a beach party, as you want something relaxed and informal. You could make a picnic with rolls and sandwiches, and hand round sandcastle buckets full of apples afterwards. I think ice lollies or ice cream cones are essential, so bring a cool box filled with cold treats for everyone to enjoy after the ceremony. You could bring cones and a box of ice cream, homemade or locally sourced, and fill the cones before handing them round, standing up in buckets.

A barbecue would also be great. Work out beforehand who will be in charge of it and how long in advance they need to light the fuel. Keep it simple, with perhaps grilled sardines or sausages, stuffed into rolls with rocket salad. Barbecued chicken, ribs and sausages will be easy to do. Hand round buckets filled with bottles of ketchup and barbecue sauce, and rolled paper napkins. If you are near a good fish and chip shop, ask someone if they can go off to buy fish and chips for everyone; it would be sensible to pre-warn the shop when you might need them to avoid delays.

Drinks

Fill cool boxes with juice boxes, fizzy water, lemonade and beer. Ask everyone to help themselves so you don't have to fuss over the guests. Have a spare bag nearby for recycling. Add a couple of bottles of sparkling wine for a toast and don't forget the cups. Glassware is probably not a great idea for a beach, in case broken glass gets left there.

Ideas for poems

- ♪ 'On the seashore' – Rabindranath Tagore (see page 173)
- ♪ 'Lullaby' – Traditional Akan poem (see page 131)
- ♪ 'I have seen …' – author unknown (see page 133)
- ♪ 'Little things' – Julia A. Carney (see page 160)

Ideas for things to say

Here are some ideas that might help you welcome your guests and make the ceremony relate to your environment.

- 'We are all here today on our favourite beach, where we have been coming since …'
- 'We chose this place as we like to be close to the sea and nature. People have always felt a strong connection to the sea, and its timeless, powerful energy, and we felt this was the right place to be today.'
- 'One of the reasons we chose to come here today is that we like to be outdoors, and we felt this was more about our family than being inside a church. We would, however, still like to share a prayer with you …'
- 'People have been coming to this beach for thousands of years and we'd like you to pause for a moment and think of all the people who have played here, swam, and had fun and adventures here.'

Holding the ceremony outside

Having the ceremony on the beach, in the garden or in a beautiful local park is a lovely idea, but of course you need to factor in the weather. If you have your heart set on being outside, then you could plan to be really flexible about when you have the ceremony. You could keep the number of guests down to a few key friends and family and, if the weather is not good on the day, change it. Or have a back-up plan for a local hall or back at home. Sometimes you just have to go for it, and be prepared to be flexible if it doesn't work out.

You could plan to hold just the ceremony outside and then head inside for drinks and food – but in the event that the weather is good, then you could have the most fantastic time! A register office celebrant will do an outside booking, but they prefer a garden or the garden attached to a hotel or other venue so that you have an alternative. The problem for them is that if you have to relocate it can take extra time to travel there and they often have several bookings in one day. If you perform your own ceremony, or ask a friend to do it, then this won't be as much of a factor.

If you plan to head to a quiet glade or a favourite spot on a beach, plan to meet your guests first at a car park or other easy-to-find place and walk to the location together. You may have put up flags, bunting or a tent in the space earlier; if so, ask a friend to stay nearby so other people don't disrupt it.

You could ask guests to bring cushions and blankets to sit on, and they can each carry drinks and food with them.

You could theme the ceremony to suit your environment and say why you have chosen it. Your friends and family will love to hear why it is personal to you and why you like to be outside, so do make it a part of the ceremony. I have heard of ceremonies held in an ancient stone circle, by a lakeside, and in a mossy grove in a wood. People often have a great affinity to nature and feel most happy and relaxed when outside, so it can feel personal and moving to be outside, especially if you choose to thank nature for the gift of your child. A Goddess naming ceremony (see page 14) would work very well outside as it gives thanks to nature and the elements.

One of the loveliest places to hold a naming ceremony is in a tree cathedral, and there are a few in the UK. Lined with hedges and containing pathways, rooms and doorways made from trees, they can be relaxing and spiritual places. Cared for by the National Trust or other organisations they are open to the public, but you could hold a small, discreet naming ceremony in one. Although concerts can be held in them, it is unlikely that you would be able to book one for your exclusive use as they are public places. You may like to hold a small ceremony in a tree cathedral, perhaps with just you and your child, and hold a larger ceremony elsewhere.

If you plan to have the ceremony in your garden or in the garden of a hotel or other venue, then you can have some real fun with the extra space. Hang up some balloons and bunting to decorate the space. You could set up a gazebo or tent to be a 'stage' for the ceremony. Move large potted plants near the stage to define and decorate it. You can arrange chairs in front of the stage for guests to sit and relax during the ceremony or you could plan to have guests standing – it is up to you. The key is to be flexible; if it is windy don't bother with the planned balloons – it doesn't matter.

After the ceremony you could all have a picnic, and there will be plenty of space for children to run around.

A marquee could be useful if you have a large group of guests and you can hold the ceremony and the party inside it. You can hire a marquee, and hotels and venues will often have good contacts and arrange this for you.

---

tips

Tips for an outside ceremony

✌ When you send invitations, include a map and directions for where you plan to be so guests can find you. Say how long you plan to wait in the car park before heading to the venue, or how they can contact you if they get lost. If you plan to be outside at home, make sure guests know to come in through a gate. Or indicate how they can find you in a hotel's grounds.

✌ Be flexible. Is it easy to set things up at the last minute, or move chairs etc. inside if you need to? Ask a few friends to help beforehand so that they come early and are on standby if you need to make last-minute changes.

✌ Letting people know your plans means they can come dressed for the weather. You could say on the invitations: 'If the weather is great we plan to be in the garden' so they come with sunhats, sun cream etc.

✌ If it is a hot day, make sure there are lots of cold drinks available for afterwards. Some fruit ice lollies for the children (and adults!) are a good option for cooling everyone down.

✌ If it is a cold day make sure there are plenty of hot drinks, and if you are going to be in a fairly remote location, ask guests to bring flasks of coffee, mulled wine or hot chocolate – and to wrap up warm!

Poems for an outdoor ceremony

Here are some ideas for poems and readings outdoors. You may also find poems relating to nature, rather than to children, which could work very well.

♪ 'Lullaby' – traditional Akan poem (see page 131)

♪ 'I have seen …' – author unknown (see page 133)

♪ Native American blessing (see page 134)

♪ 'On the seashore' – Rabindranath Tagore (see page 173)

Holding the ceremony at a register office

Only since 2008 have parents been able to hold a naming ceremony at a register office, and they may now become as popular as civil weddings. A register office can be an excellent option, as they are often beautiful local buildings and have rooms of differing sizes that can accommodate small and large groups of people. The registrar will meet with you a few weeks before so you can plan the ceremony together, choosing your vows, poems and readings. They can give you plenty of ideas and options. You can have your choice of music and they can arrange for it to be played for you.

The ceremony will be fairly short and you do have to keep to your time slot, whether your child is in the mood or not, so choose a time carefully. Most register offices do not have space for catering, so you could look nearby to see if there is a hall, café or restaurant where you could go afterwards to celebrate. Or you could state on the invitations that the party will be held at a later time at another venue and you will see the guests there. There will be time for you to have photographs outside if you like.

Some register offices have gorgeous gardens that they will be happy to let you use and they may keep a room free for you in case of poor weather – discuss it with the registrar beforehand.

Holding the ceremony somewhere different

Anything goes really, so if you want to hold the naming ceremony in your local children's farm, aquarium, zoo or theme park, then there is no reason not to! Many attractions have a meeting room or education centre that you can use. Some are now licensed to hold weddings, so they are very used to making the room look presentable. You could ask the venue's events organiser to meet with you to discuss your requirements, and they may be able to recommend local celebrants who can perform the ceremony for you.

After the ceremony, you can plan for all your guests to take a trip around the farm or zoo, which would be fantastic if you have lots of children with you. You can arrange to take a picnic or book a private dining area for food and drinks later. Many farms and zoos have animal adoption schemes so you may wish to do this as a gift to your child, and you could take the group to meet him or her!

Invitations

A clear and helpful invitation is really key for a successful naming ceremony. Many people won't have been to one before and it can help the event to run smoothly if you explain beforehand what is going to happen. Local printers and wedding invitation manufacturers will make personalised invitations for you or you can buy them ready printed for you to fill in the details. If you have a lot of information to convey, it might be best to prepare your own on a computer so you can add directions, timing, etc.

The key information to include on the invitations is:

- ❧ The date, time and place.
- ❧ The venue and address.
- ❧ What time the ceremony will take place and briefly what food and drinks will be served, e.g. "brunch at 11:30".
- ❧ Any special event that is taking place and where, for example, tree planting.
- ❧ RSVP and a date of reply.

You can include on a separate sheet directions to the venue, parking areas, places to stay and also a song sheet if you plan to have communal singing. You could also include a copy of the poems, readings and vows as guests often ask for a copy – you can do this in advance or hand them out on the day.

You could say whether you would prefer not to receive gifts, or you could suggest something special such as asking every guest to contribute to a time capsule. See page 67 for further ideas.

Ideas for decorations

Whether you are holding the naming ceremony at home or in another venue, adding some decoration will help to create a fun and relaxed atmosphere that all your guests will enjoy. There is no need to be as formal as at a wedding; you can keep your decor traditional or take inspiration from a birthday party.

Balloons

Bunches of brightly coloured balloons or balloons of one or two colours are an easy and affordable way to cheer up a room and make it look celebratory. Tie large bunches together using string or ribbon and fix them near to where the ceremony is going to take place. Balloons filled with helium (you can buy small canisters to do it yourself) will float, so you can arrange groups that are weighted at the bottom with stones or mini beanbags.

Bunting

Paper bunting is traditional at Mediterranean fiestas. You can buy long strips of white, fringed paper or make your own. To make your own bunting, measure out long pieces of string. Cut the same length of crêpe paper in your choice of colour, about 20 cm wide. Staple it along the string about every 20 cm. Carefully cut fringes along the edge, making sure you don't cut all the way to the string. Older children would enjoy helping with this. If you need to make repairs, sellotape will do the job. It won't last forever but this paper bunting looks great wrapped across trees, gazebos and along walls.

You can also make simple fabric bunting by cutting diamond shapes of inexpensive cotton. Fold each diamond in half and iron the crease flat. Fold them over a long piece of string or ribbon and make one or two stitches to hold them in place. You can reuse the bunting at birthday parties in the future. If you like, stitch or iron on letters to spell your child's name.

Flowers and ribbon

If you are using fresh flowers (also see page 103) you can coordinate the colours of the flowers. Tie small bunches of flowers on the back of chairs and tuck them into small vases or flowerpots to place on tables and near the ceremony area. You could also buy reels of thick ribbon and tie the ribbon into bunches and place it near the food and drinks tables or on the back of seats.

Fairy lights

If your ceremony or party is likely to continue into the evening, consider hanging fairy lights. You can find lights that are suitable for indoor and outdoor use. Any that you use at Christmas will work just fine. Try them out before guests arrive so you can turn the lights on with the flick of a switch as the day comes to an end. Strings of fairy lights hung around a room look great.

Chinese lanterns

Brightly coloured, paper Chinese lanterns are an inexpensive way to add decoration to an outside party. Choose the bright Chinese party colours of pink, red, yellow and cyan blue and hang the lanterns from trees and awnings where they will bob about in any breeze. You could give them to children to take home at the end of the party.

Afternoon tea party

Your party will include babies and young children and a sit-down lunch can be quite hard work for both the children and parents, so something less formal can work really well. If you provide plates of food for people to pick from when they have a moment, it can mean that they are free to move about and look after children when they need to.

Afternoon tea is traditionally served between 3 and 5 pm, so you could choose to have the ceremony at 2 or 3 pm, then have tea afterwards. The party will end at a reasonable time for parents to get young children home for bedtime, so is a very family-friendly option.

As you have the morning to get ready, you could hang up some bunting and lay out tablecloths before guests arrive to create a traditional English feel. This would work really well in a garden. If you plan to hold your ceremony at a venue, ask them if you can come in early or meet with them beforehand to tell them your ideas and to see if they can help you to create the look you have in mind. You could use several metres of inexpensive printed cotton as tablecloths. Attach them to the tables securely so young children can play near and under the tables without disaster. If you are out in the garden, put up gazebos and hang bunting from them.

Small bunches of flowers in old teapots or china cups would be an attractive and inexpensive decoration. You could pick flowers that match your cakes, such as lavender or rosebuds. If you are holding afternoon tea in the winter it will be dark at 4 pm, so you may want to light tealight candles. This would lovely but of course make sure they are placed out of the reach of small children.

For music, a pianist playing in the background would be ideal and would remind people of afternoon tea in grand hotels. Taped piano music would be great too, but choose something light and cheerful to suit the occasion.

Food

A British afternoon tea is one of the loveliest ways to spoil your guests, and it is fairly easy to organise. You will need to provide finger sandwiches, which are ideal for children and busy parents, and an assortment of small scones and cakes. Aim for a range of sandwiches, including simple cheese for young children and something like smoked salmon or roast beef for adult appeal. You can make them the night before if the bread is very fresh and if you wrap them well to keep them moist. If you provide scones, you could aim to warm them first and then serve them halved and spread already with jam and a spoonful of clotted cream on top. This saves guests having to use lots of plates and knives.

Small fairy cakes or cupcakes would be popular and easy to eat, and you can ice them in any colour you think will suit your theme. You could choose pink or pale blue icing, or stick to white, and top each cake with an icing rosebud or sweet, such as a love-heart or jelly baby. Lavender-iced cupcakes look great, and you can top each one with a sprig of fresh lavender. If you have a talented cake maker in your family, perhaps you could ask them to provide the cakes. Fruit cake is associated with traditional christenings, so you may like to provide this too. If you have kept a layer of wedding cake, now is the time to serve it.

Drinks

Large pots of Earl Grey tea would be traditional, and you could provide jugs of milk and slices of lemon. You could gather together old cups and saucers, with old-fashioned prints on them, for a traditional feel. You can often find old tea sets at sales and charity shops – they don't need to match.

English sparkling wine served with raspberries or elderflower cordial would be a lovely way to toast the child. Or you could serve Pimm's, making large jugs beforehand and filling them with lemonade and ice, and slices of cucumber and sprigs of mint or borage just before serving.

Mulled wine is a good option for a winter naming ceremony. You can make it in advance and ladle it out when guests arrive.

Ideas for poems

- 'The Tao of Pooh' (extract) – Benjamin Hoff (see page 173)

- 'Alice Through the Looking Glass' (extract) – Lewis Carroll (see page 152)

- 'Little feet' – Christina Rosetti (see page 131)

- '29 April 1989' (extract) – Sujata Bhatt (see page 172)

Ideas for things to say

- 'We chose this venue because, as many of you know, we got married here. We had such a lovely day that we thought it the perfect location for the naming ceremony today.'
- 'You may notice that the cake we have today was from our wedding, and was made by …'
- 'We have decided to hold the naming ceremony in the garden today and there is something very English about the event, which we thought you would all enjoy. We plan to plant a tree later …'

Choosing music

Using music in your ceremony or party can help to make the event personal and give it a sense of occasion. If any of your friends or family are musical you could ask if they can play or sing something. You could hire a professional musician if you prefer and if you have the space to accommodate them.

If more practical for your venue and budget, recorded music played from an iPod or CD player would work well. You could put together a playlist that suits every stage of the party. For your guests' arrival, choose calming background music that helps to make them feel relaxed. It should be quiet enough that people can talk over it.

While guests are waiting for the ceremony to start you could choose a family favourite that is meaningful to you and your child, perhaps something you listened to during pregnancy or a song that you had at your wedding.

During the ceremony you might like to listen to a particular piece, especially if you have a talented family member or older child who wants to play. You may prefer to have complete quiet at this stage. Getting everyone to sing (also see page 96) is a memorable and fun way to get everyone involved in the ceremony. You don't need to choose something serious or religious; choose whatever you like and think that everyone will be able to sing along to, such as "Bring me Sunshine" or "My Girl".

After the ceremony it is celebration time so you could choose any music you and your guests will like. Allow at least two hours of music while people enjoy drinks and food and want to chat and socialise. As you will probably have a range of ages at the party, try and include something for everyone.

Ideas for music

This is such a personal thing, but here are some ideas for music and songs that I have heard at naming ceremonies or think would make a good choice. There are some light-hearted choices and some more formal ones.

Classical options
- ♪ 'Canon in D major' – Pachelbel
- ♪ 'Let the Bright Seraphim' – Handel
- ♪ 'Champagne Aria' – Mozart
- ♪ 'O Mio Babbino Caro' – Puccini
- ♪ 'Piano Concerto No. 21, 2nd Movement' – Mozart
- ♪ 'Moonlight Sonata' – Beethoven
- ♪ 'A baby is born' – Britten
- ♪ Water Music – Handel
- ♪ 'Waltz' from 'Sleeping Beauty' – Tchaikovsky

Contemporary options
- ♪ 'You Are My Sunshine' – sung by various
- ♪ 'Bring Me Sunshine' – Eric Morecambe and Ernie Wise
- ♪ 'Imagine' – The Beatles
- ♪ 'I Want to Hold Your Hand' – The Beatles
- ♪ 'All You Need Is Love' – The Beatles
- ♪ 'I Will Always Love You' – Whitney Houston/Dolly Parton
- ♪ 'Love Is Like a Butterfly' – Dolly Parton
- ♪ 'Can't Help Falling in Love' – Elvis Presley
- ♪ 'The Wonder of You' – Elvis Presley
- ♪ 'Better Together' – Jack Johnson

♪ 'You've Got a Friend' – Carole King
♪ 'Lovely Day' – Bill Withers
♪ 'Circle of Life (from *The Lion King*) – Elton John
♪ 'Can You Feel the Love Tonight' (from *The Lion King*) – Elton John
♪ 'My Girl' – The Temptations
♪ 'A Whole New World' – from *Aladdin*
♪ 'We Are Family' – Sister Sledge
♪ 'It Must Be Love' – Madness
♪ 'Walking on Sunshine' – Katrina and the Waves

Entertainment for children

If you have a large number of young children at your naming ceremony you may like to think about some entertainment to keep them occupied. Before and during the ceremony you could provide colouring books and pencils and leave a space for toys and room to play with them. You could award a prize for the best drawing of your baby. Afterwards, depending on your budget and space, you could consider hiring an entertainer but discuss with him or her what ages the children are so there is something for everyone. A bouncy castle would also be a popular choice.

The best way to keep older children entertained is to give them a role in the ceremony, whether it is tying balloons in the garden, handing around snacks and drinks, or looking after the youngest children. You could ask one grown-up friend to think of some outdoor party games that can get them running around.

If you are planning to plant a tree or sprinkle some seeds or similar, then the children will enjoy doing that too (see page 105).

Live music, a disco or a ceilidh (barn dance) after the ceremony are good options, just in the same way as people celebrate at a wedding. Think about who will look after the babies during a long party, and allow for the fact that some people will need to head home when children get tired. If you are keen to catch up with the adults you could arrange a crêche.

Planning food and drink

Sharing food and drinks with your family and friends is a key part of a naming party, as it will bring everyone together and make it a really sociable event.

If you are using a venue such as a hotel for the naming ceremony then you can discuss beforehand what your catering requirements will be. If they are experienced at catering for weddings and parties they will have lots of ideas. There is no need to provide a formal lunch or dinner for guests – a naming ceremony is more relaxed and if you have lots of babies and children there they won't want to sit through a long meal anyway. Simple sandwiches and perhaps a special cake is more than enough. If many of your guests have a long distance to travel they may appreciate a more substantial meal so you could plan for that. Don't feel you have to though; a naming ceremony can be quite short and guests may go elsewhere afterwards for a meal.

If your naming ceremony is in a register office or at home, or somewhere that doesn't do the catering for you, then a bit of planning will help you to enjoy the day also. You probably won't have time to provide food and drinks for guests, especially if your child is still very young. You will need to do everything in advance and get help, either from family and friends or an outside caterer. Many supermarkets do events catering and you could arrange for platters of sandwiches or hot food to arrive on the morning of the party.

If you plan to organise food yourselves, then enlist the help of friends and family to help pull it all together on the day. Doing it yourself means you get control over your budget and you can choose your favourite foods. You can make it as formal or relaxed as you like. There is no need to offer formal food, as you may at a wedding. It is up to you whether you serve a barbecue, hog roast, breakfast or just tea and cakes. If you plan to organise the food and drinks yourselves, see pages 26–27 for ideas for a brunch party, afternoon tea, beach party and a winter naming ceremony.

The key is to have as much ready the day before as possible, especially if your party is in the morning or at lunchtime. Choose an easy option as many guests will also have young children and will be happy to walk about and not sit for a long time at a table. Snacks, nibbles and finger foods will appeal to children especially if they can help themselves. They may not be able to wait to eat until after the ceremony when the adults will be ready to eat, so perhaps have something easy that they can nibble on beforehand, such as breadsticks, fruit and boxes of raisins.

Main course food

Rather than finding out beforehand what guests can and can't eat, a buffet, barbecue or picnic are easy options. Put out plates of food so that guests can help themselves to what they like. Provide large bowls of salad leaves and bread so people can make up their own easy to hold lunches.

Sharing dishes, such as large baked couscous dishes, chillis, baked chicken pieces or a whole salmon, create a sociable and sharing environment which is ideal at family gatherings. You could ask family to bring one dish each to help with costs; this could take the place of a more formal gift for your child.

Desserts and cheese

There is no need to provide dessert, especially if you are serving a cake. If you like you could provide large plates of fruit such as grapes, cherries, slices of watermelon, etc. for people to help themselves to. Cheese is popular but does involve lots of biscuits, plates and knives so can be a hassle.

Baby naming cake

Cutting a cake or handing around cakes that everyone can share is a traditional way of sharing special food and helps to create a sense of occasion. You may have kept one layer of your wedding cake for this occasion or have made something new. If you have older children, you may like to make a cake with them in advance of the day, or ask them to help ice it, to get them involved. A couple of trays of cupcakes or fairy cakes, iced biscuits or gingerbread boys and girls would also be lovely options and would avoid the need for cutting the cake and using plates.

If you provide cake, there is no real need to serve dessert – coffee and cake are a lovely end to a meal. You could provide a traditional rich fruit cake, as lots of people love them, but anything goes really. The dark fruit and white icing are traditional in wedding ceremonies, but there is no similar tradition for a baby naming ceremony. Vanilla or chocolate sponge cakes may suit guests more, especially if there are lots of children present.

If you like you could add candles, and of course you would if it is a birthday cake, but there is no reason why you shouldn't also for a baby naming. You don't have to have a song but you could gather some of the younger children round to blow the candles out if it would entertain them – they love to do it!

=checklist ☑=

Food and drink checklist

☐ Work out how many plates, cups, glasses and pieces of cutlery you will need. Place them near the food so guests can help themselves.

☐ Place large jugs of water and water glasses or beakers where they can be found easily so guests can help themselves, particularly on a hot day. Cartons of fruit juice or mini bottles of mineral water would be easy choices for children, though they tend to leave them around half-finished. You could provide stickers with names on so they can find them again easily.

☐ On a very hot or cold day or if many of your guests have a long journey, then drinks on arrival will be very welcome. You could prepare flasks, coffee pots or thermal jugs of tea and coffee beforehand, and have plenty of cups nearby. Remember a bowl of sugar and a couple of jugs of milk. As you will be busy talking to guests and looking after your child, ask someone to help with the arrival drinks.

☐ People may also like a hot drink later during the party, so you may need to think about washing cups and replenishing the flasks.

☐ Have a pile of napkins nearby to hand around.

☐ On a hot day it is important to keep food cold and out of the heat so clear plenty of space in your fridge before the day, or use large cool boxes.

☐ Work out where rubbish and leftovers will go. You may like to place recycling containers nearby to help sort out the items.

☐ Plan who will clear plates and glasses left around your home during the party.

Winter party

Holding a naming ceremony during the winter months is a great idea – your guests will be pleased to have something lovely to do! A cosy room lit with candles and perhaps warmed by a real fire would be welcoming and magical. The only aspect you may need to consider is whether there will be space indoors for young children to run about. You may decide to keep the ceremony and party fairly short, especially if space inside is limited.

When guests arrive you will need space for them to leave coats, bags, umbrellas and boots. If you are in a venue, you could ask them to provide a member of staff to help with this or to set up a coat rail near the entrance, rather than expect guests to look for a cloakroom. At home, clear your coat cupboard so you have space or allocate a nearby room or bedroom for coats and bags.

Time and place

Cosy is the key for a winter ceremony. Wherever you choose to hold the ceremony and party, make sure that it will be heated and lit adequately. You may like to draw the curtains at 4 pm or ask someone to do this for you. Make sure there is good lighting, whether from fairy lights, candles or pretty lamps dotted about.

A local café or restaurant would be a good choice in the winter and they may be very happy to hire out the whole place to you, especially if it is a quiet time of year for them. If you are using a venue or hotel ask what they can do to make it cosy and special – can they light real fires and will they be protected with fireguards?

Food and drinks

Warming and filling would be popular at this time of year. You could consider warming soups, warmed bread rolls and large bowls of beef and vegetarian chillis to share. Baked potatoes that people can fill with butter, cheese and chilli would be very welcoming. If you are serving canapés you could aim for warm or hearty ones, such as toasted ciabatta slices topped with pâté and tapenades. If you are hosting a lot of guests, a hog roast would be a sociable choice. You could also do a barbecue of sausages and guests can move between inside and outside to help themselves.

If you are holding the party in the morning, then hot bacon or egg sandwiches would be a good choice and they would be easy to hold in the hand.

Plenty of hot coffee and tea when guests arrive will be very welcome, and you could serve mulled wine and hot toddies as well. You could also serve mulled wine as a toast rather than sparkling wine. If you are keen on something fizzy you could add cassis to make kirs.

 ## Setting the scene

As it is dark at 4 pm and can be quite overcast during the day, you may like to consider hanging fairy lights around the room as well as placing candles in safe locations. Candlelight gives a soft, appealing glow that creates a warm, welcoming atmosphere. Large bunches of dark flowers such as roses or dark red poinsettia plants or cyclamen look warming and are seasonal in the winter.

 Special ways to mark the day

A firework display would be an amazing way to celebrate a baby naming ceremony in winter. You can use a professional company or ask a couple of brave guests to set them off for you. Give sparklers to the children, as long as they are old enough, well supervised, and are wearing gloves. Adults would probably enjoy them too! If you have a large garden you could have a bonfire outside for guests to gather around.

A good indoor option would be to make a book of wishes, asking guests to write or draw something in a book that they would like the child to see in later years (see page 94).

Poems and readings

Here are some ideas for poems and readings that suit winter weather.

- 'I shall' – Paul Weston (see page 130)

- 'Sweet and low' – Alfred Lord Tennyson (see page 140)

- Brandon – K.L. Murray (see page 142)

- 'Lottie' – Lucy Payne (see page 142)

- 'A Celtic Blessing' – unknown author (see page 144)

Making a toast

Giving everyone a celebratory drink and asking them to toast your child is a traditional and expected way to end a ceremony.

Have glasses ready before guests arrive so they can be handed out quickly at the end of the ceremony. You can open bottles of fizz beforehand too; they won't lose any fizz in half an hour or so, but don't leave them open for much longer, especially if it is a warm day.

Decide who is going to do the toast. One of the parents would be a natural choice, or it could be your celebrant or one of your close friends or family members. Remember that everyone needs to be able to hear them. The toast could be along these lines: 'Please raise your glasses to celebrate being here today. Please join us and wish [child's name] happiness, fun and adventure.' Everyone could reply: 'Happiness, fun and adventure' or 'Congratulations'.

The traditional toast is to raise a glass of something sparkling, such as champagne, prosecco, cider or elderflower fizz. Have something that children can have too, such as lemonade or fizzy water, as they will love to join in. They could have plastic wine glasses if you prefer. If you are outdoors, everyone could toast your child with a steaming mug of coffee, hot chocolate, or a tot of whisky.

Gifts and thank yous

Guests will probably want to bring something for the child, especially if it is the first time they have met your child since he or she was born or if it is a birthday. If you really don't want gifts you could say on the invitation that there is no need for gifts. You could suggest that guests make a donation instead to a particular appeal or children's charity.

If guests do bring gifts then be available near the entrance to your venue to accept them when they arrive. You probably won't have time to open them during the party so put them in a safe place to open later. You could ask a guest to look after them for you, and take them to a safe room or car.

After the event, thank-you notes would be appreciated by guests. You could make your own or have them printed professionally, and it is a good opportunity to include a photo of your child or provide a link to a website containing photos.

You may like to give gifts to your guests as they leave as a memento of the day. This could be a small bunch of flowers, a candle, a packet of seeds or a plant in a small terracotta pot. You could wrap a piece of cake in a napkin or in an individual cake box. You can find some pretty vintage-style boxes intended for weddings, but they will work just as well for any celebration cake.

---

case study

Becca and Ceri

"We have given books to our friends' children, usually a classic or a book of poetry. In the front we write an inscription taken from the film *It's a Wonderful Life*: 'No man is a failure if he has friends.' It's something we hope they will read and understand when they are older."

If you have a lot of children as guests, they will appreciate a leaving gift, just as at a birthday party, although of course there is no obligation to do this. It can help to ease their leaving, so a small gift of a balloon, packet of seeds or cake would be well appreciated.

Naming day present ideas

If you are planning to buy a gift for the child, almost anything goes! Traditional gifts for babies include books, coral jewellery, birthstones, money boxes and silver ornaments. But with a naming day, there is no need to be tied to tradition. Here are some ideas:

Something traditional

- A classic children's book that can be read to the child now, or enjoyed when he or she is older. A first edition or one containing the child's name would be great.
- A hand-painted picture with the child's name and birthday on it.
- A chair carved or painted with the child's name.

- Offer to contribute to the child's saving account or a money box.
- Anything with the child's name on it, such as a train or book ends.
- A special quilt or blanket that the child can use every day.
- A special toy, such as a bear or doll.

Something personal

- A family tree.
- Pledge to babysit the child – this idea will be loved by the parents!
- Family photo or promise to photograph or pay for a photo session of the child.
- Painting or drawing by the giver or a professional.
- A photo frame or album containing photographs of the parents as babies.
- Lessons for the future, e.g. skiing or music lessons.
- Rose naming. You can find gift kits that enable you to name a rose and register it at the British Library. Although a lovely gift, this is not the same as a new rose being cultivated and being unique to one person, so bear this in mind.
- A small time capsule (see also page 111).
- You could sponsor an animal at a local farm or zoo for the child.
- Membership of a nearby farm or sports centre.
- A special plate and cup set.
- Tickets to a children's show.
- A DVD of a classic children's film.
- Clothes for when the child is older.
- A personalised colouring book and pencils.

CHAPTER THREE

The ceremony

Designing your own ceremony

At key moments in life, whether it is a birthday, wedding or a promotion, people naturally want to share good news with others. This can be as simple as a toast with colleagues in the office or blowing out the candles on a birthday cake. A naming ceremony can be as formal or as simple as you like, and can take whatever form feels comfortable to you. If you would like an alternative to a religious ceremony to welcome your baby and announce his or her arrival to your friends, family and community, then you can devise your own. It is not a legal requirement, so you can choose whichever words you like and are meaningful to you. If you do wish to have religious content then that is fine too; you may choose to have a religious ceremony in your place of worship and have a private ceremony at home – the choice is yours.

This chapter offers ideas for how you might structure a ceremony. You can hold a ceremony at your local register office and a registrar will help you to plan what to say, with a structure and phrases that they have found work for many people. The Humanist Society also has experienced celebrants who can lead your ceremony for you (see page 91).

In this chapter you will find an outline of what happens at each type of ceremony so you can plan ahead and work out which is going to be right for you. They are not set in stone and if there is something in particular you want to say or do, discuss it with your celebrant beforehand. You could also discuss holding a naming ceremony with your local place of worship; some churches will welcome you and do a 'blessing' which may suit you. You could then return home or to another venue to continue with readings, a tree planting or balloon release.

One of the most popular options is for parents to host the ceremony themselves, either with the help of a friend or family member, or by leading it themselves. You can write your own words and take your time over the ceremony. This can be the most relaxed and informal way to do a ceremony.

There is no set time for a ceremony. You can keep it very short and simple, with just a few words of welcome from the parents, or include more elements. It could last from five minutes to half an hour, depending on how much you say and whether you have readings and music.

Leading the ceremony yourself

Writing and leading your child's naming ceremony can be the easiest way to make it personal and unique to your family. You can keep it very short and simple with just a few words of welcome and perhaps a reading or two. You might include elements from your own beliefs or tailor the ceremony to reflect your family including older siblings and stepchildren. The information given here is only a guideline – you can devise your own ceremony or pick out elements that appeal to you. There is no legal requirement to say certain things or promises, so you can change words to say them in your own voice and move elements around.

A ceremony can contain some or all of the following elements:

● Welcome and introduction
● Reading
● Announcing the name

- Parents' promises
- Godparents'/sponsors' promises
- Reading
- Special way to mark the day
- Thank you.

A few weeks before the ceremony write out what you would like to say. You can follow one of the structures included here and pick out any phrases that appeal to you, or write your own. Practise reading it all out loud to hear how it sounds. You can also time it, so you have a good sense of how long the ceremony will take and whether you want to extend or shorten it. You can also use your written notes to remember what you want to say on the day, which is a very good idea in case nerves kick in or you are distracted by children. You could even pass it to someone else to help you on the day.

Asking someone you know to lead the ceremony

It is also a popular choice to ask a close friend or family member to lead the ceremony for you. A best friend, grandparent or even one of your older children may enjoy doing this role and can bring a lovely personal touch to the ceremony. The person you choose doesn't have to be a confident public speaker as they won't need to 'perform' to your guests, but they do need to be happy to take you all through the things you want to say and bring people forward to do readings when needed. The key is for this person to feel relaxed about doing it. It may help if they have already been to naming ceremonies, or have held one for their own child, so they know the kind of thing that is needed.

Two or more people could share the role and look after one stage of the ceremony each. For example, one person welcomes the guests, another leads the spoken part of the ceremony and a third takes everyone outside for a tree planting.

Make sure you meet up well before the ceremony so you can go through the running order and what you would like to say. You could type out the words so the person can follow a script or at least a plan of action. This can help especially if there are distractions such as babies crying or needing feeding.

The Welcome

The first thing to do is to call everyone together and to attract their attention. This is especially important if people are standing and moving around looking after children. Many people won't have been to a naming ceremony before and even if they have each ceremony tends to be unique, so it is good to outline what is going to take place. Here are some ideas:

- 'Hello everyone. We would like to start the ceremony now, so please can we have your attention.'
- 'We are here today to celebrate the birth of [child's name]. Thank you all for coming here today. It is very special to us that you are all here to share this occasion with us.'
- 'A naming ceremony is an opportunity to celebrate together the arrival of someone very special to us all. Thank you all for coming and sharing this special day with us.'
- 'Hello everyone, my name is [if adult other than parents] and it's my pleasure to welcome you here today to share

with us this very special occasion. [Mum's name] and [dad's name] have invited you all here today to celebrate the arrival of [child's name]. They want to officially welcome [child] into their family, and to the wider family of relatives and friends. Everyone here is very important to the family, and we/they look forward to your continuing friendship, interest and involvement throughout [child's name] life.'

Introduction

This is when you outline what will happen in the ceremony so guests know what to expect. It also reminds you of what you plan to do! This is helpful as guests can work out how long it will take, when to keep children as quiet as possible and when they might need to move outside. As baby naming ceremonies are new to many people, and often take different formats anyway, telling everyone what will happen can help to relax guests and set the tone of the event. You don't need to ramble on explaining every detail but mentioning the key elements will be helpful.

- 'Our ceremony will be short and simple. We plan to say a few words about [child's name] and make promises to him/her. [Sibling's name] would then like to read a poem.'
- 'Some of the family will be joining us with readings and poems, and [name] is going to sing a song. It would be great if you could all join in if you'd like to, and we will hand around the words.'
- 'After the ceremony, we'll go outside for lunch and champagne, and later we plan to plant a tree.'

First reading

As soon as you have introduced what is going to happen, you could have your first reading or poem. Perhaps choose a confident adult to start with so they can set the tone and energy of the ceremony. You can choose anything you like, but perhaps something quite general about children and new life would be suitable at this point. Introduce the person who is to read the poem, and why you have chosen both the reader and the poem.

- 'We have asked [name] to read [title of poem or reading]. We have chosen this because …'
- 'The first poem we have chosen involves us all. As a community of friends and family we all share a responsibility to provide the atmosphere in which young [child] will develop as a person.'

tips

- Keep your head up and speak slowly.
- Practise speaking or reading in front of someone before the day so you can work out what you feel comfortable with.
- If you are distracted by your child for a moment, pause until everyone is focused again before re-starting.

Announcing the name

This is one of the key points in a naming ceremony. Although the guests will know what your baby is called, it is part of the ceremony to announce your baby's full name, including any middle names. You can prolong the length of this element by explaining why you chose the name. This can be an interesting and enjoyable part, as guests often don't know the reasons behind the name. At a recent naming ceremony I went to, one grandparent was delighted to learn that the child had a middle name after her. I heard that one baby's name 'Kai' is associated with water and dolphins, which is a connection between the parents – and he was born in water!

- 'We would like to introduce you all formally to [child's name]. He is brother to [siblings' names] and we are all very pleased to welcome him to our family.'
- 'We would like you all to meet [child's name], the newest addition to our family. He is surrounded today by grandparents, aunts, uncles, cousins, brothers and sisters, and we all feel very lucky that he is with us today.'
- 'As you all know this is [child's name]. Would you all like to give three cheers/raise a toast to welcome her to our family.'
- 'We chose the name [child's name] because …'
- '[Child's name] was born on [birth date] at [location]. We knew when we saw her that she suited the name [child's name] and we wanted to choose a family name too, which is why we named her after Grandma. One year on and we can see already that they share the same sense of humour, as well as the same lovely brown eyes.'
- 'We have also found out that the name [child's name] means … and we very much hope that proves to be true.'

Parents' promises

As everyone has settled, now is a good time to say any personal thoughts and promises that you would like to share. It can work well if a celebrant or friend asks you 'questions' to which you as parents reply. Or you can simply say your thoughts and promises directly to your child. One or both of you can speak, or you could take it in turns. You can make this part quite formal, as if making wedding vows, or keep it simple. Choose whichever makes you feel most comfortable.

During a wedding both partners make promises to each other about their commitment to each other, and you can take this idea and adapt it for your naming ceremony. Pledges and promises are also a key part of humanist and civil naming ceremonies. You can choose promises from the ideas here or you may like to make your own.

Sit down with your partner before the ceremony and think about what is important to you. You don't have to come up with an exhaustive list – just two or three key points will be enough. You may decide that what you want to do as parents is raise your child in safety, and yet with fun and adventure in his or her life. You may want something fairly formal, or feel more comfortable saying something relaxed. You may also like to repeat your wedding vows if you feel they are appropriate, or make a promise to each other as parents that you will love and support each other while you raise your child together.

● 'We would like to take this opportunity to promise to [child's name] that we will be the best parents that we can.

We promise to love you, to look after you, and care for you as long as you need us.'

- 'We would like to say thank you for the gift of our baby. He is very precious to us and we promise to take the very best care of him.'
- 'I promise to help bring as much fun, laughter and silliness into your life as we can. We want to be your parents and also your friends, so we hope to have lots of fun together.'

Some of the questions to which you could respond with promises include:

- 'Do you promise to care for [child's name] and help him/ her to grow up to be happy and contented? Nurture his/her curiosity, courage and enthusiasm so he/she can challenge life with confidence?'
- 'Do you promise to offer warmth and shelter and keep him/ her safe, and allow your child his/her own identity, thoughts and opinions?'
- 'Do you promise whenever possible to meet his/her needs, dreams and desires? Do you promise to help teach him/her right from wrong, and always offer a good example on the journey from childhood into responsible adulthood?'
- 'Do you promise to try to bring up your baby in a home filled with kindness, tolerance, patience and love and help him/her to fulfil his/her true potential?'
- 'Do you promise to be there in times of need, to offer your comfort, support, friendship, love and understanding whenever your child needs you?'

You can also make promises to each other as parents, for example:

● 'I promise to support you as we raise [child's name] together. I promise to share in tasks and jobs and to do my share of night feeds!'

● 'I promise to do my best to give [child's name] a safe, loving and caring home, and to share with you the responsibility for that.'

Godparents'/sponsors' promises

If you have decided to include special adults in the ceremony, you could introduce them now. You could say that they are not going to be called godparents but are going to have a special role in raising the child. You could give your reasons, although there is no need to do so.

● 'We would like to ask [names of special adults] to come to the front. We have asked these two to act as godparents/sponsors/ fairy godparents as they have always been there for us, and we would like them to be involved in [child's name] life.'

Your special adults don't need to say anything. They can simply stand at the front with you and be involved in the ceremony later on, perhaps by leading a balloon release. Or they may like to make some promises to your baby:

● 'I/We would like to promise to be there for [child's name] and he or she can always turn to us for help if ever needed.'

● 'I/We promise to help and support [parents' names] with moral support or practical help as they raise [child's name].'

Second reading

If you have older children who would like to be involved in the ceremony this would be an ideal opportunity to include them. They could read a poem or reading of their choice, or one that they have written themselves. A family member or friend could also do a reading for you. If you are in a particular venue or location, such as on the beach or in the garden, perhaps choose something that is appropriate to this setting. You might like something more light-hearted than the first reading, or more formal – the choice is yours.

Music and singing

If you have musical friends or family members, then ask them to play or sing at the end of the ceremony. Music has the power to move people in an amazing way, and can help to bring focus and a sense of a special occasion to the ceremony. Most people enjoy singing and don't often get the chance. If you choose a song that people know and provide copies of the words, you might be pleasantly surprised that they join in.

- ♪ 'We have asked [name] to sing for us, so please sit down and make yourselves comfortable before she starts.'
- ♪ 'We love to sing and as this is such a happy occasion we have chosen a song that we think you will all know. So if you would like to join in, we will just hand out the words now. It is [song title].'

Special ways to mark the day

This is an opportunity to do something to celebrate the occasion, such as cutting a cake, planting a tree, releasing balloons or watching a fireworks display. There are many things you can do (see Chapter 4 for ideas) and you can include as many as you like. You could cut a cake inside or have a champagne toast, and then ask guests to move outside for the special event. Explain what you are going to do so guests are in the right place at the right time. You can also say why you are doing it.

- 'We would like everyone to go out to the garden now as we would like to scatter some seeds to make a wildflower garden for [child's name]. We hope that he or she will enjoy it in years to come and watch the plants grow. You can help us to make this happen.'
- 'Please can everyone move outside now and we will hand each one of you a balloon. Please hold on tight to it until we tell you otherwise!'
- 'We would like to plant a tree that will grow as [child's name] grows. We have chosen an apple tree, as we hope that he/she will look after it and pick the apples in the future.'

Ending the ceremony

Just before you all move outside or go to eat and drink, it is a good idea to end the ceremony in some way. This can be short and simple but it is important as otherwise you can have guests hanging around not quite sure of what to do with themselves.

- 'For those among you with religious views we would like to add that this ceremony will in no way inhibit [child] from seeking religious knowledge and answers in the future. We would like to give him/her the choice in the future to find out for him/herself.'
- 'We would like to say one final thing to [child's name]: may life's richest joys be yours. May you grow to be happy and healthy and to live life to the full.'
- 'We would like to say that we are all here to help you in life, and to share life's fun and adventures with you.'
- 'We have now finished the naming part of the ceremony. We will hand around glasses of fizz so we can raise a toast to [child's name].'
- 'We would like to thank you all for coming and for sharing this day with us. Please stay and enjoy some food and cake with us.'

A wedding naming ceremony

As a wedding is a legal ceremony, it will be led by the registrar. Before the wedding you will meet with your registrar to go through the ceremony and you will be able to choose the promises you would like to make to each other. At this meeting you should also be able to go through the naming ceremony and identify any promises you would like to make to your child and to each other as parents.

If you would like to arrange this part yourselves, here are some ideas for things to say:

- 'We would like to thank you all for coming today and for celebrating our marriage. There is another important person here today, and we would like to take this opportunity to welcome him/her into our family and make promises to him/her too …'
- 'We/Do you [parents' names] promise to care for [child's name]? Do you promise that you will give him/her a safe and loving home?'
- 'We/Will you promise to introduce your child to friendship, fun and adventures?'
- 'We/Will you promise to make [child's name] a valued and loved part of your family?'
- 'We/Will you promise to comfort him/her when he/she is tired or sad, and join in with laughter when he/she is happy?'

Ideas for poems

- ♪ 'The tie that binds' – Eileen Ellis (see page 132)
- ♪ 'Through baby's eyes' – Author unknown (see page 130)
- ♪ 'I shall' – Paul Weston (see page 130)

Birthday party ceremony

If you want to combine a naming ceremony with a birthday party, here are ideas for special things to say:

- 'We would like to welcome everyone to [child's name] first birthday party and naming ceremony. We have decided to combine the two as this is a wonderful opportunity to have so many friends and family together.'
- '[Child's name] is now old enough to enjoy the ceremony a little more – and we have had time to recover from his/her arrival!'
- 'There will be lots of toys in a little while so all the children can enjoy themselves, but first we would like to take a few moments to hold a short naming ceremony for [child's name].'

Ideas for poems

- ♪ 'Now this is the day' – Zuni Indians (see page 133)
- ♪ 'It's your birthday' – John Maguire (see page 150)
- ♪ 'My first birthday' (see page 146)

What happens at a register office

If you hold your naming ceremony at a register office, or ask a registrar to come to your home or chosen venue, the order of ceremony will be very similar to one you might lead yourselves. The main difference is that the registrar will lead the ceremony and promises will be made in the form of question and answer, much in the same way as a wedding. This can help to prompt you and give the ceremony structure and gravitas. When you book a civil ceremony you will meet beforehand with a registrar to go through the order of the ceremony and to choose promises. You can keep it quite short or add more elements such as readings and music. After each question, the parents respond with 'We will' or similar.

A naming ceremony is the civil equivalent of a christening. The child's name is confirmed and the parents declare promises to their child of their commitment to giving him or her a caring and loving home. Other adults make promises to support the parents in both physical and moral aspects of life. For everyone involved, making these promises publicly gives them more weight and importance. If the child is lucky enough to have grandparents, they too may make promises to assist in the upbringing of the child.

In order to incorporate all these aspects, there are various choices of phrases and promises for you to choose from and put together into a formal ceremony. It is nice to add some readings to the ceremony, expressing the sentiments that you wish for your child. If one or more of your guests read these, it can be a very personal and meaningful to you and your family. Music may be included in the ceremony also, either at the beginning and end or as part of the ceremony.

Civil naming ceremonies may be held anywhere that is suitable. You may hire a licensed venue or use a village hall, your own garden or a marquee. Because there is no legal aspect to this ceremony you are not tied to a particular venue or form of words, although the ceremony is conducted by an experienced celebrant from the registration service.

Here is an example ceremony from a register office. The registrar will open the ceremony and bring everyone's attention that it is due to start. Here are some of the phrases that he or she may say:

- 'Hello everyone, my name is [registrar's name] and it's my pleasure to welcome you here today to share with this family a very special occasion.'
- 'We meet here to take part together in a simple ceremony. We do so for a number of reasons. Firstly, [parents' names] wish to express their joy to you on the birth of [child's name]. They are pleased that [child] has arrived safely in this world. They want to welcome him/her into their family, to the wider family of their relatives, and to the community of their friends.'
- 'They wish you all to share this joy. It is certain that the more love a child receives the more he/she will benefit in his/her life and the more love in turn he/she will be able to give to others. So your presence at this celebration today is appreciated, as will be your interest and involvement in the years ahead.'
- 'The parents would like to make promises to [child's name] and then we will have a reading from [name]. We will then introduce the supporting adults. We will then join in together to sing a song that the parents have chosen, before raising a toast to [child's name].'

Including the parents

One of the first things a registrar will do is turn to the parents and ask them to introduce the baby to the guests. This can be short and simple with an announcement of the name. Parents can then make promises to the child, much in the same way as a wedding promise. You can choose what you want to say and a celebrant will have ideas to help you make that decision.

- 'What name have you chosen for your child?' [The parents announce the chosen name/s.]
- 'Your name was chosen with great care, and it was chosen just for you. Your name is special to you, just as you are special to us.'
- 'Will you the parents care for [child's name], give him/her a safe, warm and loving home?'
- 'Will you introduce your child to friendship, fun and adventures and let him/her grow? Will you care for [child's name] so that he/she feels loved and secure, as best you can?'
- 'Will you comfort [child's name] when he/she is distressed, and join in with fun and laughter with [child's name] when he/she is happy?'
- '[Dad's name] and [Mum's name] wish to express their joy in the birth of [child's name], and they want to officially welcome him/her into their family unit, and to the wider family of relatives and friends. [Dad's name] and [Mum's name] would like you all to share their joy on this happy occasion, and they also look forward to your continuing friendship, interest and involvement in the years ahead.'
- 'A child brings his/her own unique personality, and adds a new dimension to the family unit. [Dad's name] and [Mum's name] will always find something new to laugh at or admire. [Dad's name] and [Mum's name] are also aware of the great responsibility that is now theirs. A great deal of their lives will be involved in caring for their child and guiding [child's name] through the many trials of life.'
- 'Names are an important part of everyone's life, and names

are what give each and every one of us individuality. Parents please stand: [Dad's name] and [Mum's name], what name have you chosen for your child?'

● Speaking to child: '[Child's name], your name was chosen with great care, and it was chosen just for you. We all hope that you will inherit the best traits of [Dad's name] and [Mum's name] and grow into a caring person who is healthy and happy, and with wisdom to help you all through life.'

● 'I'd now like to ask the parents to make promises. [Dad's name] and [Mum's name], will you as parents care for [child's name], keep him/her clothed, sheltered and protect this child for as long as he/she needs you, as best you can?' – Parents respond: 'I/we will.'

● 'Will you try to raise [child's name] so that he/she will feel loved and secure?' – Parents respond: 'I/we will.'

Including siblings

If you already have children, it can be very meaningful for them and for you to include them in the ceremony. It depends on their ages, but even the youngest child can be brought forward to say something or simply to be included. Older children may like to say or read something, or even write their own promises. Very young siblings can be included if you keep them alongside you throughout the ceremony, and perhaps by them giving a small gift to the baby.

● 'I'd now like to ask [sibling's name] to come up to the front to be with us. [Sibling's name], here is your baby brother/ sister. Will you try to be kind to [child's name] and help look after him/her?' – Sibling responds: 'Yes.'

● 'Will you also try to have lots of fun and happy times together? Try to treat each other as you would wish to be treated. You will be brothers/sisters for ever and this is a very special bond that only you share.'

● 'Will you be kind and help look after him/her and surround him/her with love and affection?' – Sibling responds: 'Yes.'

● 'Will you comfort [child's name] when he/she is sad and laugh with [child's name] when he/she is happy?' – Sibling responds: 'Yes.'

---

case study

Elena, Megan and Ruby

'We decided to have a Thanksgiving ceremony for our children. We also didn't want to ask friends to be godparents who were non-believers and yet would be asked to make certain promises. What we did want was something to publicly announce and celebrate the arrival of the children. I wanted to thank God for them and it was therefore important for me to mark the occasion in a church, and a Thanksgiving seemed the right choice.'

Including supporting adults (godparents)

Traditional 'godparents' are members of a church group who promise to help support the parents in the spiritual growth of the child. There is also the more modern factor that parents name someone in their will who will care for their child in the event that they are unable to do so. There is no reason why you cannot include these important people in your ceremony. You don't have to give them a special title, but you could choose from 'supporting adult', 'godparent', 'sponsor' or even 'fairy godmother'. A humanist celebrant would probably prefer a more formal approach, but what you call them in your own time is up to you.

🖐 'The next special and unique step in this ceremony involves the godparents. In this age of the nuclear family when many of us live isolated from our family and friends, godparents have perhaps a more important role today than they have had in the past. They undertake a special and lifelong interest in the welfare of their godchild and assume a more than ordinary responsibility in the event of the death or default of the parents. So, I now ask the godparents, are you, [name] and [name], willing to accept this serious charge?' – Godparents respond: 'We are.'

🖐 '[Parents' names] have chosen [names] to be supporting adults/godparents/ sponsors for [child's name]. They are chosen because …'

🖐 'Supporting adults should be willing to take a special and lifelong interest in the happiness and development of [child's name]. Do you promise that you will be there for [child's name] and that he/she can turn to you in the future for loving support and guidance as he/she grows?'

🖐 'The bond between parents and their children is very strong, but the support and encouragement of others is vital for the development of a child. [Dad's name] and [Mum's name] have chosen [names] as supporting adults/ godparents for their child for whom they have the highest regard. Supporting adults/godparents should be willing to take a special and lifelong interest in the moral and ethical development of their godchild.'

🖐 'Will you accept this commitment and responsibility?' – Supporting adults/godparents respond: 'I/we will.'

Including grandparents

If you would like to include grandparents in the ceremony, the registrar can help you to do this. Bear in mind that family members of an older generation are more likely to expect or prefer a religious ceremony, so discuss what you plan to say or do beforehand so everyone feels comfortable.

- 'It is not always possible for grandparents to help with the raising of their grandchildren, but when they do it is a great bonus and blessing. The important role played by grandparents is the passing on of cultural values to children.'
- 'Being a grandparent can be a special role. A child can learn their history and family traditions. Grandparents often also have lots of fun with the children as they don't have the same lack of sleep!'
- 'We have asked [grandparent's name] to say a few words about what it is like to be a grandparent ...'
- '[Grandparent's name] would like to read a poem about what it is like to be a grandparent.'
- '[Child's name] is very lucky to have four grandparents and we are looking forward to them all being involved with his/her future.'

Finishing the ceremony

It is a good idea to finish the ceremony in some way just so guests know it is finished and they can move away, or move to where the drinks are! If you plan to finish with a song or a piece of music, tell people so they know what to expect. The registrar could introduce the song or music and tell guests what is going to happen next – for example, ask that you all join in and then go outside, or that after the song he/she will say a few more words. They may even help you raise a toast, but this tends to be more appropriate for the parents to do when the formal part of the ceremony is over.

- 🌿 'This ceremony today will in no way prevent [child's name] from seeking future religious commitments or beliefs. The parents have given [child's name] the freedom to choose for himself/herself in the future.'
- 🌿 'We all hope that [child's name] will have a happy, exciting and fulfilling life.'
- 🌿 'I have pleasure in presenting to you: [child's name].'
- 🌿 'On behalf of the parents I would like to thank you all for taking part in this ceremony. The plan is now to move outside to the garden for photos and drinks.'

A Humanist Society ceremony

The Humanist Society can lead a meaningful and well-structured ceremony for you, and they have the experience to keep the ceremony flowing. The Humanist Society has helped lead weddings and funerals for many years and you may have family contacts with a particular celebrant or be used to humanist ceremonies. The idea is that a humanist ceremony is based on the support and community values of people, without religion.

Freelance celebrants

You can find freelance celebrants who can lead the ceremony for you. When you meet a celebrant he or she will give you a copy of the words that can be said in a naming ceremony and you can adapt it to suit your own wishes. You may have some choices to make, and you can make the ceremony short or introduce poems and readings. If you would like to include your own words, then discuss this with the celebrant beforehand and he or she will help you work them in.

CHAPTER FOUR

Special ways to mark and remember the day

Doing something special

A naming ceremony is usually quite short, which is a good thing when you have lots of babies and young children present. You can lengthen the ceremony and also bring originality to the event by marking the day in a special way. There are plenty of lovely things that you can do on the day such as planting a tree or scattering some seeds. You could also do something beforehand, such as naming a star, which you can tell guests and your child about in the future. You can hold the more formal part of the ceremony first, have a break, and then continue with a special event such as a tree planting or a balloon release. You can also make the event even more sociable by getting guests to join in with filling a time capsule or singing a song.

A best wishes book

This is a similar idea to the books that are sometimes passed around guests at a wedding, and it is a very easy and interesting way to remember the day. It is also a fun way for guests to participate in the event. You provide a large blank book and pens so that guests can write a message to the child. It can be anything they like, from a simple hello to their personal thoughts on the occasion. You could provide coloured pencils so that younger guests can draw a picture. Hopefully, after the party, you will have a special keepsake of the day and everyone there.

You will need to buy or make a large blank book. Choose one with plenty of space on the pages, and with paper that can be written on easily with pen or pencil. Fix a good pen with ribbon to the book, to avoid people asking for a pen throughout the party. You might like to stick a piece of paper on the front that says, 'Please feel free to write your thoughts, advice, best wishes etc. in here so we can read it to [child's name] when he/ she is older'. Make sure you can remove this piece of paper after the party. You could personalise the cover afterwards with photographs of your child.

A good way to encourage people to write in the book is to start it off yourself. Glue photographs of your child and family in the book and start to add notes about the day, such as the date, guest names, details of readings etc.

Place the book in a place that people can find easily, such as near the food or gifts. You could ask a friend or family member to pass it round later in the party, as you will probably be too busy to do this yourself.

After the party, add any ephemera from the day. This could include photographs, pressed flowers, greeting cards, gift tags etc.

Getting everyone involved

People like to be involved in a ceremony, so don't be afraid to ask them to join in with some parts. There will be times when guests need to listen but you can also get them involved by bringing something to the event, joining in with a toast or singing a song. Here are some ideas:

● When each guest arrives, give them a postcard or photo of the child on which you have written a dream, wish or hope for the child. For example, 'I hope that [child's name] gets to travel the world and have lots of adventures' or 'I wish that [child's name] grows up to be kind, happy and fulfilled'. At a point in the ceremony, ask each person to read their card out loud.

● Give everyone candles when they arrive and during the ceremony ask everyone to light them, passing the lit flame from one to the next.

● Singing is a great way to involve everyone in the ceremony, but you will have to provide words. 'You are my sunshine', and 'Bring me sunshine' are good, fun choices that most people will be able to join in with.

● Ask guests to bring something to put in a time capsule for your child to open in the future.

● Ask guests to bring a copy of their favourite children's storybook to create a library for your child. You may get a lovely mix of new and classic books.

● Move everyone outside to scatter seeds in the garden, or together plant a tree or smaller plant and water it.

● Take part in a balloon release together. Rules for balloon releases require you to stagger the letting go of the balloons, so the children could release their balloons first followed by the adults.

Singing together

People do love to sing and just because you are not holding your naming ceremony in a church or other place of worship there is no reason why you cannot enjoy a song. If you have musical family and friends, ask them to play at the ceremony – this can bring a lovely personal touch. You could project words onto a wall or hand around sheets printed with the words. If you choose a familiar song, then there is no need to provide the words; guests will be able to sing along. You might ask one or two confident friends to get you started, perhaps by singing loudly or singing the first verse before others join in.

'Bring Me Sunshine'

Bring me sunshine, in your smile,
Bring me laughter, all the while,
In this world where we live, there should be more happiness,
So much joy you can give, to each brand new bright tomorrow,
Make me happy, through the years,
Never bring me, any tears,
Let your arms be as warm as the sun from up above,
Bring me fun, bring me sunshine, bring me love.
Bring me sunshine, in your eyes,
Bring me rainbows, from the skies,
Life's too short to be spent having anything but fun,
We can be so content, if we gather little sunbeams,
Be light-hearted, all day long,
Keep me singing, happy songs,
Let your arms be as warm as the sun from up above,
Bring me fun, bring me sunshine, bring me love.

Words by Sylvia Dee
Music by Arthur Kent

'You Are My Sunshine'

You are my sunshine, my only sunshine
You make me happy when skies are grey
You'll never know dear, how much I love you
Please don't take my sunshine away.

Words by Gene Autry

Making the ceremony personal

There are many ways to make your child's naming ceremony unique to your family. Small touches can really make the event memorable and give guests something to talk about and remember afterwards.

- Choose music that was special to you during your pregnancy or the birth.
- Serve food that you particularly liked during pregnancy. One of my friends really loved olives during her pregnancy, so she served them at the ceremony.
- If you have talented people in your family, such as someone musical or someone who loves to perform, then ask them to play, sing or read.
- If you have older children or close family with children, ask them to read a poem or sing a song, or draw a picture that could go on the invitation.

Handprint art

Tiny handprints are a really evocative reminder of how small your children once were, so this is a great opportunity to make a piece of art that you can keep for years. You could print your child's handprint on a stretched canvas, to be mounted straight on to the wall, on paper to be framed or on a plate or plaque to hang on the wall.

You could print just your child's hand or footprints, or include the handprints of all siblings together. One option is to collect the handprints of all the child guests that come to the party, using an A3 sheet of paper or a large canvas and asking them to fill the space. You could write the names next to each handprint. When it is dry, frame the picture to protect it from wear and tear if you need to – and you have a great reminder of the day and some art for your child's bedroom.

Specialist pottery painting shops are widespread and they sell blank pieces of pottery, including plates, plaques, cups and moneyboxes that you can print on and add personal details to such as a name and birthday. They will glaze and fire your piece of art for you, which will protect it for years. Allow at least a week for firing if you want it ready for the naming day. You could also buy a kit from the shop complete with plate or plaque and paints, and decorate it with handprints on the day. Take it back to the shop for glazing and firing, and then collect it when finished.

Ready stretched and primed canvases are widely available from art supply shops. Use any water-soluble emulsion paint to ensure it adheres to the canvas. Try to find a non-toxic paint and do wash your child's hands quickly afterwards. A 'box' canvas can be hung straight on to the wall and doesn't need to be varnished or protected in any way.

---

tips

Tips for painting

- Choose a washable, non-toxic paint and paint on to the child's hand using a soft paintbrush. It is quite difficult to open a young child's hand, so be ready with the paper; you may need to bring the paper to the child.
- If you're including more than one child, do the youngest first and ask the older children to print around it. If you have lots of young children it may be better to use paper rather than a canvas so you don't mind if it takes a few sheets of paper to get it right.
- Don't worry about the odd splodge of paint or missing thumb; this adds to the charm, and you can always add a little more paint to complete a print if required.
- Have plenty of wet wipes or a damp towel to hand, and wash the hands quickly and thoroughly to avoid children getting paint in their mouths or on any passing guests or furniture.

Balloon release

Just after the ceremony you could ask each guest to release a balloon. This can make a lovely conclusion to a ceremony and is very appealing to children. You could choose colours that match your cakes and flowers, or your child's favourite colour, and you could print photos or words on the balloons. There are environmental concerns with releasing a lot of balloons, so please stick to these guidelines:

- Only use natural latex rubber balloons, not ones made from foil as they will not biodegrade. Tie the balloons with flax string or simply knot them; don't tie streamers, ribbons, labels, or anything that won't break down easily, to the balloons.
- Use helium gas to inflate the balloons so they float high enough to burst and disperse properly.
- Release the balloons one by one rather than all at the same time to let them disperse in the air gradually.
- If you plan to release 5,000 or more balloons you need to get approval a month in advance from air traffic control and local authorities (see page 178).

Sky lanterns

Release paper lanterns as an alternative to a balloon release. Each paper lantern can be decorated beforehand, and you could write your child's name and date of birth on them before release. Or if you have lots of children at the naming ceremony, you could provide soft crayons or paint pens and paper stickers for them to decorate the lanterns. When you are ready, light the bottom of the lantern. The warm air inside the lantern will make it rise into the sky and, as it will burn, it will not create too much litter.

Photographs, DVDs and videos

These are all excellent ways to record the naming party. Here are some tips to help get the results you want:

- Ask a friend or family member to take photographs or a recording for you; you and your partner will be too busy looking after your child, guests and trying to enjoy yourselves to take lots of photos. Don't forget that guests will want photographs of you with your child and you will need to be available for this.

- You may choose to hire a professional. If so, first check the style of images he or she produces and discuss beforehand the type of shots you want. Let him or her know what you plan to do on the day so they are prepared for indoor and outdoor lighting. You could provide a list of key family members so you get shots of the people you want.

- Bear in mind that babies and young children can find flash photography upsetting so try not to take too many photos, and tell guests kindly if your child has had enough. To keep older children entertained, you could provide them with disposable cameras – you could get some very interesting shots!

- If you feel very strongly that you do not want too many photographs and recordings taken in case it upsets your child or takes up too much time, then add a short note to the invitations. You could say that you will organise for photos to be taken and will make them available to everyone online after the event.

- After the naming party, you could send digital images to an online printing company. You can have professional albums printed at a very reasonable cost, or a favourite image enlarged and framed.

● The key to a good photo album or video recording is to edit. Cut out any shots of people at strange angles or standing looking lost.

Flowers

Seasonal flowers given as a gift or used to decorate the venue are a gorgeous, personal touch. You may like to use flowers as a theme and find or make invitations with a flower motif. If you plan to hold some of your ceremony outdoors, you could ask guests to plant bulbs or plants so that they are in season when it is your child's birthday.

Here are some of the flowers that are in season throughout the year, so you can choose a flower that you will be able to find.

January	Snowdrop (*Galanthus*)
February	Primrose (*Primula vulgaris*)
March	Daffodil (*Narcissus*)
April	Tulip (*Tulipa*)
May	Globe thistle (*Echinops*)
June	Cornflower (*Centaurea cyanus*)
July	Rose (*Rosa*)
August	Poppy (*Papaver*) or Sunflower (*Helianthus*)
September	African blue lily (*Agapanthus*)
October	Hydrangea (*H. quercifolia*)

November	Cyclamen (*C. hederifolium*)
December	Holly (*Ilex*) and Mistletoe (*Viscum album*)

Planting bulbs or plants or scattering seeds will appeal to adults as well as children. You could even give a planted bulb as a 'going home' gift for guests. You can find small terracotta plant pots in garden centres for no more than £1 each. Fill the pots with all-purpose compost and pop a bulb in each one. You could label the pot or write on it with chalk, with the name of the plant and the planting date as well as details of the naming ceremony.

Planting during the ceremony

To organise a planting outside, make sure you include on the invitations what you plan to do so that your guests can wear the right footwear and bring coats if needed. Prepare an area of the garden before the ceremony so it is ready for the planting. You could give every child a bulb, small plant or a few seeds to scatter around. If you want to, make up small packets or bags of 'fairy dust' with oats and a tiny amount of glitter that children sprinkle over the earth when the planting is finished. You may need to cover the seeds or bulbs with more soil to plant them properly, and protect them from birds and small animals.

You may like to make a small sign that you hang up nearby to mark the occasion, and your child can water the plants and visit them over time.

Planting trees

One of the most popular ways to mark the occasion of a naming ceremony is to plant a young tree that will thrive and grow along with your child. You could plant this in your garden, or in a nearby wood or park. Many local councils have tree planting schemes and will even provide a plant. You could also ask at your local nature reserve. If your local park operates a scheme, you may be able to plant a tree where your child is likely to play when he or she is older – that way, you can visit your special tree and lots of other children will benefit also.

There are urban planting schemes, so if you live in a city without a garden you can still do a planting and take your child to visit the tree. You also know that you have done something to improve the environment of every local person. The Woodland Trust (see page 179) organises tree planting schemes in their own woods and their excellent website provides advice on which trees to choose and how to plant them properly.

Forested areas and national parks often have organised schemes where you sponsor a tree, rather than plant it yourself. If you choose this option, you are making a very positive contribution to your community by helping to restore an area, and you will be able to enjoy walking or picnicking there with your child in the future. You will be able to explain what you did and perhaps ask him or her to pick the tree in the forest they like the best. Schemes often provide a certificate, which you can add to photographs of the naming day.

If you plan to plant a tree in your garden, choose one that will look interesting all year round. One that produces fruit such as apples or plums tends to be more appealing and interesting to a child. Choose one that will bear fruit as soon as possible so you don't have to wait for years. Some fruit trees need to be planted in pairs to cross-pollinate, so check with your local garden centre before you buy. Some have really beautiful flowers or blossom in the spring, stripey bark, or fruit, conkers or catkins in the autumn. Or choose a tree or plant that has a name similar to your child's, such as jasmine, holly etc. If you are a family of nature-lovers, you could find out which trees particularly appeal to wildlife and birds.

Consider also the size of your garden and check the tree's maximum growing height and width to make sure it will fit in your space without crowding out other plants. You might like to think about how long you plan to stay in your home; if you will be there for just a few years, choose a small, fast-growing tree so that you can see it at its best before you move. Even if you move earlier than expected, other families will enjoy your tree and you will have provided a habitat for nature.

As your tree grows, take photos on the anniversary of the naming ceremony or your child's birthday, perhaps with your child alongside so you chart how they grow together.

If you plan to add a tree house, platform or swing, ask advice at your local garden centre about how long the tree will take to grow to a good height and strength. You can buy trees that are two to three years of age, which will help speed things up. You could start with a rope swing and add to it as the tree and child grow. You can buy attractive wood swings and engrave the child's name on it. If you want to add a bench around the trunk, find out what the tree's width will be and allow space for it to grow.

tips

Preparation tips

❶ Dig the hole for the tree before any guests arrive. Make sure it is deep and wide enough. Water the hole well. Cover the hole with a hard cover and place the tree nearby to warn people where the hole is.

❷ Remove any wrapping or tags from the tree. You might like to wrap the trunk of the tree in ribbons or fabric, ready for when guests arrive.

❸ Place a shovel, extra soil and a watering can nearby, ready for planting the tree when it is time.

❹ You might be able to find or make a small plaque to place on or next to the tree to say that this is your child's special tree.

Favourite trees

🌿 **Magnolia:** This tree has gorgeous pink and white blooms. It grows at a low height for many years, meaning that it is a very child-friendly size!

🌿 **Fruit trees, including apple, damson and cherry:** Each of these trees has blossom in the spring and delicious fruit in the autumn. Imagine how lovely it would be to pick the fruit with your child from their special tree.

🌿 **Chestnut:** If you have the space for a chestnut tree, your child will love conkers and their spiky shells and you can teach him or her to play conkers when older. Future generations will be able to add a tree house or swing.

Tree symbolism

As trees are strong and last for many years, often outliving the people who plant them, they are associated with many meanings:

- **Olive:** In Roman times the olive leaf was a symbol of abundance, glory and peace. It was offered to kings and deities and to the victors of athletic games. Olive oil was considered sacred when used in ceremonies.
- **Oak:** A symbol of strength and endurance, the oak is the national tree of many countries including England, France, Germany, Poland and the United States. Several individual oak trees are of great historical or cultural importance. In Celtic mythology the oak represents doors and gateways between worlds. There are numerous proverbs about the oak as an inspiration for living, such as 'Mighty oaks from little acorns grow' and this would be a good inscription for a plaque or sign placed near the tree.
- **Fig:** In the Old Testament the fig tree was a symbol of prosperity and security. The Bodhi tree under which the Buddha gained enlightenment is held sacred in India.
- **Maple:** North American storks use maple branches in their nests which means that the maple is now associated with love and a new child in the home.
- **Apple:** In folklore, mythology and religion, apples appear as a mystical or forbidden fruit. It is also associated with domestic comfort and home-cooking!
- **Clover:** The shamrock, a clover with three leaves, is the symbol chosen by St Patrick to represent the Holy Trinity. Ancient Celts revered the clover and had many beliefs based on triads. Clover's sweet smell is said to induce

calm and contentment. It is also thought to be lucky.

Lily: The lily is often associated with whiteness, purity of heart and innocence. In China the day lily is the emblem of motherhood and also symbolises harmony.

Rose: For the Ancient Romans and Greeks, the rose symbolised love and beauty. The rose is the national flower of England and the US. You can find varieties of rose that share the same name as your child. Naming a new rose is often a very expensive procedure, but you can find varieties with appealing names that you can choose (see page 179).

Daisy: This flower opens and closes with the sun, so has the name 'daes eage'. It is associated with childhood innocence, simplicity and modesty.

Thistle: The thistle is an ancient Celtic symbol of suffering as well as strong character and birth.

Sunflowers

If you have children already, you might like to help them plant sunflower seeds so that they feel involved in the day. Or you could send all child guests home with their own packet of seeds!

Create a special place to play

If you have a large garden you could allocate one part of it as a gift to your child. This could be a playhouse, a den made from sunflowers, a sandpit … If you have mature trees in your garden, you could 'give' one tree to your child, and add a special wrap-around bench, swing or tree house. You could carve his or her initials and the special date.

Candle lighting

Lighting a white candle is a traditional, symbolic part of a christening ceremony, but there is no reason why you cannot include candles in some way in a naming ceremony if you choose. Candlelight is very evocative, and is a part of many modern rituals such as birthday cake candles, as well as playing a more prominent role in pagan ceremonies.

If you want to include lighting a candle, with or without words of explanation, go ahead. At some point during the ceremony, perhaps towards the end, you can include a candle lighting moment. You could either light one special candle yourselves, or ask a sibling or cousin to do so which can help other children in the family to feel involved. Alternatively, you could ask every guest to light, either a small tea light or a handheld candle. This would look amazing if you are holding a winter naming ceremony, especially if it is dark. You might prefer to keep it simple and at low danger risk by simply having candles lit on a mantelpiece or table out of the reach of small hands, bringing a sense of warmth and light to the occasion.

Ideas for words to say

- 'Lighting a candle symbolises to us new life and new hope for the future, and perhaps when family and friends light candles in their home they may pause to think of all the friends and family gathered here today.'
- 'We have asked [sibling's name] to light a candle as a special way to celebrate her brother's naming day. She has said that she would like to do this every year and light the candles on his birthday cake for him.'
- 'Supporting adults, [name] and [name], please light your candles from [child's name] candle. Repeat after me, 'As I light this candle, I confirm that I am part of [child's name] personal family. [Child's name] may always turn to me for guidance, comfort and love.'

Fill a time capsule

Instead of traditional gifts you could suggest that your guests bring something that can go in a time capsule, or you can fill it yourselves. This can give your child an evocative snapshot of the year he or she was born. This is a really easy and interesting project to do, and you can involve older siblings by asking them to collect things to put in the capsule. The idea is that you choose a large box or container to store your items, and plan to open it when the child is older, say on their eighteenth birthday. Choose a container that will last for this length of time and you will need to think of a safe, dry place to store it. Some companies supply lead or stainless steel capsules that can be buried safely in the garden, which is a fantastic way of making sure that no one opens it before time. But you could use any airtight container and store it in the loft if you prefer, making it easy to take it with you when you move.

Ask guests to bring something: you could end up with a real variety of interesting items that, although commonplace today, will be good fun to look through in 18 years' time. It is entirely up to you what you choose to put in the time capsule, but here are some ideas to get you started:

- A naming day invitation and copies of the poems and readings you chose.
- A list of everyone who came to the naming ceremony, and a photo and story about them.
- Photographs of your child/children, you and your partner, family members, friends and pets. Black and white photographs retain picture quality longer than colour ones. Be aware that at the moment, Polaroid photographs could decay over 18 years.
- Drawings by siblings and friends.
- A CD of the family's favourite music.
- A video or DVD of the naming day.
- Small toys and favourite items of baby clothing.
- Hospital wrist band and delivery notes, if you have finished with them.
- A shopping receipt to show the price of items in that year.
- Local property paper showing the house prices that year.
- A newspaper from the same date as the naming day or birthday of your child.
- A magazine to show the fashion and food tastes of the year.
- Family tree.
- First-day cover collection of stamps.
- A collection of coins, with one of each denomination.

- A chart compilation CD to show the music tastes of the year.
- A copy of the child's favourite book.

It is important that everything you put in the box is spotlessly clean. You may even like to wear gloves when you place items inside to help avoid any dirt and grease getting inside the capsule, which can lead to items decaying before you are ready to open the capsule.

Don't put in anything perishable, such as food, flowers or toys made of rubber or containing batteries, as these can lead to the decay of other items too. Hair and wool items may also give off a gas as they decay which may damage items.

You can use special archival ink if you plan to write notes or include children's drawings in the capsule. This will last longer than regular ink or felt tip. If you plan to include a CD, video or DVD, bear in mind that technology will change in the future, so you may like to update it at a later stage. Each item should be placed in a separate polythene bag before going in the capsule to protect them.

Storing the capsule

Placing the capsule in a dark cupboard or loft space should be fine, and it means that you can find and take it easily if you move house. It is good fun to bury the capsule in the garden and this could be a great thing to do on the actual naming day itself, involving siblings and guests when you bury it. If you plan to do this, dig the hole in advance. Just remember to dig it up if you move house.

You could mark the location of the capsule in some way, perhaps by placing a small metal or stone plaque on top of the capsule site or on a nearby wall.

If you choose to store the capsule indoors, choose a place that is rarely disturbed and that is dark and dry. Try to protect it from fluctuations in temperature, so don't store it close to a water tank, for example.

You may choose not to open the capsule yourself, leaving it for future generations to discover. The International Time Capsule Society keeps a register of time capsules and registering your child's capsule may help to protect it in the future.

---

case study

Bea's time capsule

'We asked guests to bring something that we could put into a time capsule. Bea received things like a shopping receipt, local and national newspapers, coins ... Bea's older sisters wrote a poem and drew pictures of her. She has something truly unique that she can open perhaps when she is 18.'

Sponsor a child

Many parents would like to organise something special for their child that celebrates their naming day. This does not need to happen on the actual naming day or be presented in any way. Sponsoring a child in another country or naming a star, for example, are projects that you can start when your child is a baby and talk about throughout his or her childhood. Grandparents, siblings and godparents may like to do this also, as a special, personal gift.

Sponsoring a child from the developing world who has a less fortunate background can be a life-long commitment. Several well-organised charities can arrange this for you, making the process easy and rewarding. You can pledge as much as you can afford and just a few pounds a month can make a difference to a child's life. Your sponsorship can be the difference between a child attending school or working from a very young age.

As your child grows, you can tell him or her about the sponsored person, which is a wonderful way to educate him or her about the world. You may be able to request to sponsor a child similar in age to your own and with a similar birthday.

Sponsored children have a range of backgrounds and problems, but many are caused or made worse by poverty. Sponsorship can help with food, clean water, clothing, healthcare, education and skills training. Often sponsorship money goes towards funding projects in the local community to help with long-term projects such as water supplies or growing food. The sponsored child benefits, as does the whole community, by becoming more self-sufficient. Some organisations focus on providing support to children who have lost their parents and to help them find new homes, sometimes within the child's village.

Hearing from the child

Most sponsorship organisations will provide you with details of the child and his or her community, yearly updates, photographs and letters about how the child is progressing. This way, you and your family can see the difference your support makes. This may be a personal letter from the child, and you may be able to write back. This could be a very valuable way for your child to connect with someone elsewhere in the world. Some organisations will tell you the sponsored child's upcoming birthday, so you can send a card. You may even like to visit the child. Many sponsors have found this to be very rewarding and have become part of their lives, but this is entirely up to the individual sponsors.

case study

Our experience of sponsoring a child

Sponsoring a child has many benefits to both parties, as one parent explains:

'I visited the SOS Children's village in, Madras, India, when I was a newly qualified teacher. It was different from the surrounding area; here the children had space, toys, access to education, food and a family of children and caring helpers.

When I returned to England and started a family of my own I was very conscious of the privileges that my own children would take for granted, that compare so starkly with the conditions I remembered from my visit to India. I wanted my children to know about other children and the lives they led, and I wanted them to care about the plight of those less fortunate.

We have had the privilege of watching Arjun grow up. Every year he writes to us, and we write back to him. He sent us pictures and we reciprocated. Now he is nearly grown up and on his way to independence.

It is my belief that if every family in the developed world sponsored a child in the developing world, then we could, on a micro-level, achieve what the G8 summit is attempting on a global scale. And it is of minimal financial impact on our affluent societies.'

Name a star

An unusual, creative way to remember the naming day is to name a star for your child. You can choose a star in a constellation, for example in Andromeda (Princess) for a girl, or in Ursa Minor (Little Bear) for a boy. A star listing company will record your child's name on a register and will provide you with the star's telescopic coordinates and information about what time of year you can view it. They will provide a chart showing the location of the star and a gift certificate that registers the star with your child's name.

Every star in the sky falls into one of 88 different areas known as constellations. Constellations are named after many things, including animals, zodiac signs and creatures from Greek mythology. You can choose which constellation you want your star to appear in and can make it relevant to your child, such as his or her zodiac sign.

Some stars are visible all year round, whereas others are visible only during certain months, so choose a star that is visible either during the month of your child's birthday or naming day. For example, Andromeda (Princess) can be seen all year round, but Delphinus (Dolphin) can only be seen between May and

November. Very few stars are visible to the naked eye so you will need a telescope to view it.

You will need to make sure that the constellation you choose can be seen from your location in the world. If you live in the UK, for example, choose a constellation that can be seen from the northern hemisphere.

The only official body that can actually name a star is the International Astronomical Union (IAU), and no individual person can actually 'own' a star. Most stars are known by a catalogue number and very few are named after individuals. However, as a beautiful and symbolic gift, star naming is a lovely way to celebrate a naming day and will appeal to children for many years. When your child is older you can enjoy spotting the star together, which is also a wonderful way to introduce a child to astronomy.

How to name a star

Many companies provide a star naming service and will make the process easy and enjoyable (see page 179). They will also provide a gift certificate and a map to show the location of the star.

❶ Choose a name for your star. This is usually the child's name but it could be a special nickname or family name.
❷ Decide if you'd like the star to appear in a specific constellation.
❸ Check that the star can be seen from the country you live in, and at what point in the year.
❹ Choose an official registration date, which will appear on the gift certificate. This could be the child's birthday or the date of the naming day.

Constellations

All these constellations can be viewed from the UK, although some are only visible during certain times of the year:

- Ursa Minor (Little Bear)
- Equuleus (Little Horse or Foal)
- Perseus (Hero)
- Leo Minor (Little Lion)
- Andromeda (Princess)
- Cygnus (Swan)
- Delphinus (Dolphin)
- Columba (Dove)
- Eridanus (River)
- Grus (Crane or Stork)
- Gemini (Twins)

Give your child the moon

For a bit of fun, you could buy your child a piece of the moon! Apparently, American Dennis M. Hope spotted a loophole in The Outer Space Treaty of 1967, and filed a declaration of ownership for the Earth's Moon on 22 November 1980. He has been selling acres of the moon ever since! Each gift pack comes with a lunar map, showing you where your acre is located. If this doesn't appeal, perhaps you would prefer an acre of the red planet, Mars, or Venus, which is one of the brightest objects in the night sky. This would certainly be a fun gift especially for older children – or you could start saving up for a space flight.

Astrologically, the moon is associated with the emotions, changing moods and the ability to react and adapt to other people and a range of different environments. The moon is yin, feminine, maternal, receptive and represents the need for security. In mythology Artemis, the twin sister of Apollo, represents the moon, and is also the defender of children.

Shells

If you plan to hold your naming ceremony on a beach you may like to know that shells are often used in ceremonies. A scallop shell is used during a christening and is a symbol of baptism. It is often used to pour water over the child's head.

A conch shell is one of Buddhism's Eight Auspicious Symbols and represents the power of the Buddha's teachings. Hindu culture and some island cultures used the conch as a musical wind instrument.

Adopt an animal

If you or your children are animal lovers, why not adopt an endangered or rescued animal as a special way to celebrate your baby's naming day? You could choose to bring an animal home from a pet rescue centre, but if you don't have space or think that your child is too young to have a pet around, you could adopt a zoo or rescue centre animal that you can visit.

Adopting an animal is something that most zoos and rescue centres do, as it is a great way to bring in extra funds. You help to fund their work and you may help to protect animals that, otherwise, may not be around when your child grows older. You can choose to sponsor almost any kind of animal, including a sea horse, donkey or lion. As this is to celebrate your baby's arrival in the world, why not choose to sponsor a baby animal? The cost varies according to the size of animal, as the larger ones need more food. In return you will be sent a certificate, a photograph of your animal and regular updates. To make the animal adoption part of the naming ceremony, you could find a soft toy that matches the animal and give it to your child – you can explain why at a later date.

Some zoos fund rescue centres elsewhere in the world. For example, Bristol Zoo supports a primate rescue centre in Cameroon, West Africa where they help to rescue apes from the bushmeat trade. By adopting an individual animal, you will be directly helping to feed and care for it until it can return to a safe place in the forest. The World Wildlife Fund (WWF) offers adoption of wild animals located in a project area funded or run by the WWF, in the animal's home country. You could also consider sponsoring a local pet rescue centre, which provides homes for abandoned cats and dogs. This is a great idea if you don't have space to have a pet at home, but would like to help.

You may like to adopt an animal to take home and pet rescue centres can provide a vaccinated, neutered animal. However, it is probably best for everyone concerned if you wait until your child is older and you have more time to care properly for the pet.

If you would like to bring a pet home, have you thought about rescue chickens? You can find chickens that have been raised in battery farms and you can bring them home to live in your garden. You need only the smallest garden – when you think about the space they have lived in before, even the smallest yard will feel like luxury. You need to make sure they are secure in their run at night so they don't get attacked by foxes. As they return to health they can become good egg layers, and your child can learn all about where eggs come from and how to care for another creature.

Animal symbols

When choosing an animal to sponsor you may like to consider some of the folklore associated with it:

- **Dog:** Emblem of faithfulness and guardianship. Dogs embody courage, playfulness and sociability. They are often found on crests.
- **Cat:** Associated with independence, confidence and wisdom. Has magical connotations. A Japanese Maneki Neko (beckoning cat) is a ceramic figure believed to bring good luck.
- **Rabbit:** Fertility, innocence and youthfulness. In China and Japan rabbits are associated with the moon and the Chinese moon festival. In North America a rabbit's foot is carried as a charm on key rings for good luck.
- **Lion:** Strong but gentle. A symbol of courage, majesty and prowess.
- **Tiger:** In Asia a tiger represents royalty, fearlessness and wrath. In Tibetan Buddhism a tiger represents confidence, kindness and modesty.

- **Elephant:** Because of their abilities, the elephant is a sign of wisdom in Asian cultures. Admired for memory and high intelligence.
- **Bear:** Associated with strength, cunning and ferocity in protection of its family.
- **Monkey:** Courage, perseverance, selflessness and devotion. In the Chinese zodiac people born in the year of the monkey are often inventors, entertainers and the creative mind behind any undertaking. Also symbolise intelligence and the ability to solve problems.
- **Mouse:** Because mice live so near to the ground they are believed to have a close relationship with earth spirits and ancestors.
- **Butterfly:** Symbolises human frailty and the ephemeral nature of life.
- **Dragonfly:** For North Americans dragonflies represent swiftness and activity. They are said to symbolise renewal after periods of hardship. In Japan, they are symbols of courage, strength and happiness.
- **Bee:** Associated with hard work and fidelity. In many cultures bees have been thought of as messengers of the spirits. In Celtic lore they represent the wisdom of the other world. Also associated with immortality and can be found on tombs.
- **Spider:** Symbolises resourcefulness, mystery, power, growth and rebirth.
- **Duck:** Because they glide on the water, ducks can symbolise superficiality, chatter and deceit, yet also gracefulness and friendliness. A pair of ducks in Chinese and Japanese cultures represent marital happiness and fidelity.

Stork: Because they are devoted to their offspring, storks are symbols of good parenting. In Bulgarian folklore the sighting of a stork returning from its winter migration is a sign of spring.

Peacock: This beautiful bird is associated with mercy, paradise and immortality.

Owl: Thought of as wise, this nocturnal bird is a symbol of wisdom, intelligence, mystery and secrets.

Dolphin: People are attracted to the dolphin's intelligence, grace and smile. A dolphin is a Christian symbol of Christ guiding souls to heaven.

Birthstones

Jewellery is an unusual gift for a young child, but you may choose to give a birthstone to be worn when the child is older. You can also find stones set into silver boxes which can be a lovely keepsake for baby teeth, or special gifts and toys. Coral was used as a christening gift in Roman times and is still a traditional choice as a gift for christenings. You may find your child's birthstone would also make a great first or middle name.

January	Garnet
February	Amethyst
March	Bloodstone/Jasper
April	Diamond/Sapphire
May	Emerald
June	Pearl/Agate
July	Ruby/Turquoise

August	Carnelian/Agate
September	Sapphire
October	Opal
November	Topaz
December	Turquoise/Ruby

Symbolism of stones

🌿 **Ruby**: Associated with love and power. In Christian lore a ruby is considered an emblem of good fortune, banishing sorrow and negative thoughts. It is also a healing stone that combats exhaustion and imparts vigour. It brings about a positive and courageous state of mind and promotes enthusiasm for life.

🌿 **Coral**: This marine organism is associated with christenings. Ancient Romans put red coral necklaces and bracelets on their children to protect them from danger. Today in many cultures red corals are still worn as a talisman to protect the wearer from the 'evil eye'. In China coral is a symbol of longevity. Red coral is one of the five sacred stones of the Tibetan Buddhists and symbolises the energy of the life force. Tibetans and Nepalese think of coral as a good investment and they believe that the person who wears coral will be successful in life.

🌿 **Amber**: This fossilised resin has been appreciated since ancient times for its colour and beauty. It is considered a powerful healer and cleanser of the body and environment. Amber absorbs negative forces and stimulates positive ones that bring healing and balance to life.

Garnet: Travellers used to carry garnets to light up the night and protect them from disaster. It has been found in early jewellery from Egyptian, Greek and Roman times. Today garnet is thought to be a powerful, energising and regenerating stone. It helps self-perception.

Topaz: A symbol of beauty and splendour. It is thought of as a bringer of joy, generosity, abundance and good health. It can help to support the achievement of earthly goals.

Emerald: The Incas and Aztecs of South America regarded the emerald as a holy gemstone. The green of emeralds is the colour of life, springtime, beauty and enduring love. It also symbolises inspiration and patience.

Sapphire: Every shade of blue sapphire symbolises sympathy, harmony, friendship and loyalty – everything that is constant and reliable. In the East it is regarded as a charm against the 'evil eye'. The stone is said to promote tranquillity.

Diamond: Represents purity and the bonds of a relationship. Associated with strength, courage and integrity.

Quartz: Symbolises balance and perfection. As a healing stone it is considered a master healer, perhaps the most powerful stone on the planet. Quartz generates strong vibrations that cleanse the organs and balance the subtle bodies. It helps to absorb negative energy and helps the balanced expression of emotion, thought and desire. It is also said to enhance psychic abilities and the immune system.

Moonstone: This soft milky white stone resembles the colour of the moon. It is a sacred stone in India where it is claimed that the moonstone can lead to psychic immortality.

Pearl: Associated with all that is feminine and symbolises purity and perfection. In the modern day it means a rare thing, for example wisdom.

CHAPTER FIVE

Poems and readings

Selecting poems

There are many lovely poems that you can include in your baby naming ceremony, from the classic and serious, to the more light-hearted. This chapter includes only those that are suitable for reading out loud, and that are relevant to babies, young children and naming ceremonies.

You could choose a poem that resonates with your views on parenting and the importance of children in society, or simply one that you think your guests will enjoy listening to. A classic poem could be read by a parent, grandparent or a special adult you have chosen, and you could choose an easier, more humorous poem for a sibling to read out.

I have included a couple of poems that refer to God and heaven, and these may be suitable if one of the parents or grandparents hold religious views and would like to include a religious reference in the ceremony. There is no reason why you cannot; as long as you are not holding the ceremony in a place of worship, or with a Humanist celebrant you are in charge of the content.

tips

♪ Send a copy of the poem to the reader well before the ceremony so he or she has a chance to practise reading it out loud. Let them know roughly when you plan to ask them to read it, whether at the beginning or end of the ceremony, so they can be ready.

♪ When choosing a poem, read every line carefully to check that there are no hidden surprises, such as a reference to something sad, or something clearly meant to be an adult romantic poem.

♪ Time yourself or your friend reading the poem out loud. It needs to be short to keep everyone's attention so you may choose to read just one verse or a favourite passage from a poem, but check that it continues to make sense

♪ If you need to, change some of the words of the poem, or miss out a verse or line. Change the words 'he' to 'she' and vice versa. If you think the poem is too long for the person reading it, then do feel free to cut it. You could introduce the extract by saying, 'This is taken from the poem …'

♪ The reader needs to stand near the front so that they can be heard by everyone. If guests are sitting, the reader can stand where they are, if you prefer. You could ask that they check that everyone can hear them before they start. Look up as you read so guests can hear every word.

♪ Practise reading the poem, letting someone listen to you so they can point out anything that is not clear or easily understood.

♪ Underline or highlight any special parts of the poem or reading to remind yourself to give them more emphasis when reading out loud.

♪ Guests often ask for a copy of the poems and readings, so you might like to print out some copies to hand out afterwards. You could include them in a simple order of service that you hand out on arrival.

Poems for adults to read

Through baby's eyes
Author unknown

I didn't expect a brass band, with welcome mat unfurled.
To be on hand when I arrived, in this confusing world.

Nor did I expect a Doctor, to hold me by the feet,
then quickly turn me upside down, and spank my on the seat.

At first I wasn't quite prepared for this enormous place,
nor for the funny characters, that I would have to face.

But I soon learned to get my way, by looking sweet and shy.
And when I wanted to be held, to make a fuss and cry.

I've found it really doesn't take much difficulty or guile,
to wrap them around my finger;
All I need to do – is smile.

I shall
Paul Weston

I shall shield you from the darkness,
I shall ease your worldly fears,
I shall hold you warm and tender,
I shall wipe away your tears.

I shall walk beside you hand in hand,
I shall dry you from the rain.
I shall lead you to a rainbow,
I shall keep you from your pain.

I shall stay with you forever,
I shall be a shining light.
I shall give my heart completely,
I shall comfort you at night.

I shall smile each day you're with me,
I shall share a love so deep.
I shall store this love within my soul,
This love within to keep.

Little feet
Christina Rosetti

Little feet, too young and soft to walk
Little lips, too young and pure to talk.

My baby has a mottled fist,
My baby has a neck in creases;
My baby kisses and is kissed,
For he's the very thing for kisses.

Lullaby
Traditional Akan poem

Someone would like to have you for her child
but you are mine.
Someone would like to rear you on a costly mat
but you are mine.
Someone would like to place you on a camel blanket
but you are mine.
I have you to rear on a torn old mat.

Someone would like to have you as her child
but you are mine.

(*African Poetry*, ed. Ulli Beier, Cambridge University Press,
1966.)

The tie that binds
Eileen Ellis

Yours and mine in equal measure
This child or ours, our living treasure.
Before him we were just a couple,
Now the bonds between us double.
Mine to him and his to you,
The three of us, not just we two.

We watch him in his cradle sleep
With so much love we almost weep.
We'll watch him grow into a boy
Bringing us both tears and joy.
We'll watch him grow into a youth
And bring him up in light and truth.

We'll watch him grow into a man
And love him as only we two can.

I have seen...
Author unknown

I have seen a mother at a cot – so I know what love is;
I have looked into the eyes of a child – so I know what faith is;
I have seen a rainbow – so I know what beauty is;
I have felt the pounding of the sea – so I know what power is;
I have planted a tree – so I know what hope is;
I have heard a wild bird sing – so I know what freedom is;
I have seen a chrysalis burst into life – so I know what mystery is;
I have lost a friend – so I know what sorrow is;
I have seen a star-decked sky – so I know what infinity is;
I have seen and felt all these things – so I know what life is.

Now this is the day
From the writings of Zuni Indians

Now this is the day,
Our child,
Into the daylight
You will go out standing,
Preparing for your day.

Our child, it is your day,
This day.
May your road be fulfilled.
In your thoughts may we live,
May we be the ones whom your thoughts will embrace,
May you help us all to finish our roads.

Native American blessing

Sun, Moon, Stars, all you that move in the heavens, hear us!
Into your midst has come a new life.
Make his/her path smooth, that he/she may reach the brow of
the first hill!

Winds, Clouds, Rain, Mist, all you that move in the air, hear us!
Into your midst has come a new life.
Make his/her path smooth, that he/she may reach the brow of
the second hill!

Hills, Valleys, Rivers, Lakes, Trees, Grasses, all you of the earth,
hear us!
Into your midst has come a new life.
Make his/her path smooth, that he/she may reach the brow of
the third hill!

Birds, great and small, that fly in the air,
Animals, great and small, that dwell in the forest,
Insects that creep among the grasses and burrow in the ground,
hear us!
Into your midst has come a new life.
Make his/her path smooth, that he/she may reach the brow of
the fourth hill!

All you of the heavens, all you of the air, all you of the earth, hear
us!
Into your midst has come a new life.
Make his/her path smooth, then shall he/she travel beyond the
four hills!

May all your wishes come true
Unknown author

May all your wishes come true.
May you always do for others, and let others do for you.
May you build a ladder to the stars and climb on every rung,
And may you stay forever young.
May you grow to be righteous,
May you grow up to be true,
May you always know the truth, and see the light that's
surrounding you.
May you always be courageous, stand upright and be strong,
And may you stay forever young.
May your hands always be busy, and may your feet always be swift.
May you have a strong foundation when the winds of change shift.
May your heart always be joyful, and may your song always be sung,
And may you stay forever young.

Hello baby
Becky Alexander

A new baby changes everything;
Life will never be the same;
Sleep seems a distant memory,
Ever since your baby came.

But every time you look at her,
It does all seem worthwhile,
You know that you would never go back,
Every time you see her smile.

Follow Your Dreams

Jim Boswell

When others say 'It's hopeless and it really can't be done.'
When they tell you 'It's all over. It's a race that can't be won.'
And they promise 'You could spend your life just lying in the
sun.'
Follow your dreams boy. Follow your dreams!

When the people you admire, but who wouldn't understand,
Tell you 'Other roads are safer. Your dreams are much too grand.'
Or the doubters and the tempters try to take you by the hand.
Follow your dreams boy. Follow your dreams!

You should listen to the counsel of the people that you trust.
But don't be turned aside just because they might get fussed
You live the life that in your heart you know you really must.
Follow your dreams boy. Follow your dreams!

There is nothing you can't conquer if you believe you can.
No mountains you can't straddle, no oceans you can't span.
Just conjure up a vision and set yourself a plan.
Follow your dreams boy. Follow your dreams!

Advice to Small Children

Edward Anthony

Eat no green apples or you'll droop,
Be careful not to get the croup,
Avoid the chicken-pox and such,
And don't fall out of windows much.

Wishing you many smiles
Unknown author

Wishing you many smiles and happy times to come.
May life's adventures be exciting and sweet,
Filled with love from the friends that you'll meet.
You'll soon grow up for time does fly,
So cherish each moment as it goes by.
From crawling and walking
To toddling and talking
There's no knowing what you'll do next.
There's a threshold to cross and a wide open door,
And a wonderful world for you to explore.
Sleep with the moonbeams and play in the sun,
Let your life be a long one and filled with fun.
May today and tomorrow and all days hereafter,
Be days that are happy and filled with your laughter.

For my grandson
Brenda Blackbell

From the moment I saw you
I adored you sweet child.
From the moment I held you
My heart was beguiled.
So small yet so perfect.

A grandson to treasure
To love you so purely,
Will be my great pleasure.
To watch you grow older

To see wisdom thrive,
My life has new meaning
Now you are alive.

For my grandson
Hazel Williams

Who do you look like, new little child?
You looked like your father
As soon as you smiled.
You're a bit like your granddad;
A lot like your mother
And, from certain angles,
Like your older brother.
You're not like your aunty;
You're nothing like me, but
You carry our genes and
Now we can all see
That though you're your own person,
With a life of your own,
You'll take us all forward with you,
When you're grown.

Infant joy
William Blake

I have no name:
I am but two days old.
What shall I call thee?
I happy am,

Joy is my name.
Sweet joy befall thee!

Pretty joy!
Sweet joy but two days old,
Sweet joy I call thee:
Thou dost smile,
I sing the while,
Sweet joy befall thee!

(*The Complete Poems*, Penguin Classics, 2004.)

Frost at midnight (extract)
Samuel Taylor Coleridge

Dear Babe, that sleepest cradled by my side,
Whose gentle breathings, heard in this deep calm,
Fill up the interspersed vacancies
And momentary pauses of the thought!
My babe so beautiful! It thrills my heart
With tender gladness, thus to look at thee,
And think that thou shalt learn far other lore
And in far other scenes! For I was reared
In the great city, pent 'mid cloisters dim,
And saw nought lovely but the sky and stars.
But thou, my babe! Shalt wander like a breeze
By lakes and sandy shores, beneath the crags
Of ancient mountain, and beneath the clouds.

(*The Complete Poems*, Penguin Classics, 2004.)

Monday's child
Unknown author

Monday's child is fair of face,
Tuesday's child is full of grace,
Wednesday's child is full of woe,
Thursday's child has far to go,
Friday's child is loving and giving,
Saturday's child works hard for a living,
But the child that is born on the Sabbath day
Is bonny, and blithe, and good, and gay.

(First recorded in A. E. Bray's *Traditions of Devonshire*, 1838)

Sweet and low
Alfred, Lord Tennyson

Sweet and low, sweet and low,
Wind of the western sea,
Low, low, breathe and blow,
Wind of the western sea!
Over the rolling waters go,
Come from the dying moon, and blow,
Blow him again to me;
While my little one, while my pretty one, sleeps.

Sleep and rest, sleep and rest,
Father will come to thee soon;
Rest, rest, on mother's breast,
Father will come to thee soon;
Father will come to his babe in the best,

Silver sails all out of the west,
Under the silver moon:
Sleep, my little one, sleep, my pretty one, sleep.

(Published by Penguin in various editions)

Cradle song

Alfred, Lord Tennyson

What does little birdie say
In her nest at peep of day?
Let me fly, says little birdie,
Mother, let me fly away.
Birdie, rest a little longer,
Till thy little wings are stronger.
So she rests a little longer,
Then she flies away.

What does little baby say,
In her bed at peep of day?
Baby says, like little birdie,
Let me rise and fly away.
Baby, sleep a little longer,
Till thy little limbs are stronger.
If she sleeps a little longer,
Baby too shall fly away.

(Published by Penguin in various editions)

Brandon
K.L. Murray

You brought a ray of sunshine
When all around was grey
I don't know what would have happened
If you hadn't come our way.
You put a spark of love and hope
In our hearts filled with grief and pain
You made us laugh, where once we cried
Made us want to live again.
Now you fill our days with love
And happy dreams at night
You came, a gift from up above
Our special guiding light.

Lottie
Lucy Payne

Your smile radiates
Like a ray of hope in my darkened world
Awakening hidden hopes, revisiting forgotten dreams

And I return the gesture
My lips lifting gingerly at the corners
A Cheshire crescent transforms my features

The sight of a child's joyful face
Is all I need
To brighten my spirits
And keep me going
All through the day.

To Ianthe

Percy Bysshe Shelley

I love thee, Baby! For thine own sweet sake,
Those azure eyes, that faintly dimpled cheek,
Thy tender frame, so eloquently weak,
Love in the sternest heart of hate might wake;
But more when o'er thy fitful slumber bending
Thy mother folds thee to her wakeful heart,
Whilst love and pity, in her glances blending,
All that thy passive eyes can feel impart;
More, when some feeble lineaments of her,
Who bore thy weight beneath her spotless bosom,
As with deep love I read they face, recur –
More dear art thou, O fair and fragile blossom;
Dearest when most they tender traits express
The image of thy mother's loveliness.

Rainbow on the moon

Andrew Hobbs

There's a rainbow on the moon tonight
It's there
It's just for you,
It's there to take your treasured hand
And there to lead you through.
Seek it when you're feeling lonely
Let it lead you to your dreams
Fall into its arms tonight
Caress its wish-filled beams
It's yours

It always will be
I put it there myself,
I put it there with loving grace
And a wish for worldly wealth.

May beauty delight you
Unknown author

May beauty delight you and happiness uplift you,
May wonder fulfill you and love surround you.
May your step be steady and your arm be strong,
May your heart be peaceful and your word be true.
May you seek to learn, may you learn to live.
May you live to love, and may you love – always.

A Celtic Blessing
Unknown author

May the strength of the wind and the light of the sun,
The softness of the rain and the mystery of the moon
Reach you and fill you.
May beauty delight you and happiness uplift you,
May wonder fulfil you and love surround you.
May your step be steady and your arm be strong.
May your heart be peaceful and your word be true.
May you seek to learn, may you learn to live,
May you live to love, and may you love – always.

We loved you from the very start
Unknown author

We loved you from the very start,
You stole our breath, embraced our hearts.

Our life has just begun,
You're part of us my little one.

As mother with child each day you grew,
Our minds were filled with thoughts of you.

We'd dream of the things we'd like to share,
Like late night bottles and Teddy Bears.

Like first steps and skinned knees,
Like bedtime stories and ABCs.

We thought of things you'd want to know,
Like how birds fly and flowers grow.

We thought of lessons we'd need to share,
Like standing tall and playing fair.

When we first saw your precious face,
We knew your life would be touched with grace.

We thanked the angels from above,
And promised you un-ending love.

Each night we lay you down to sleep,
We gently kiss your head and cheek.

We count your little fingers and toes,
We memorise your eyes and nose.

We linger at the nursery door,
Each day we realise we love you more.

Through misty eyes, we dim the light,
And whisper, 'we love you' every night.

We loved you from the very start,
You stole our breath, embraced our hearts.

My first birthday
Unknown author

Just 12 short months ago I made my big debut
So now I'd like to celebrate my first birthday with you.
My little hands play pat-a-cake, they peekaboo and wave
They catch me while I learn to walk and splash me when I bathe.
They hold your fingers tightly and touch your heart so deep.
My little hands reach out to you for hugs before I sleep.
My little hands are tiny but yours will serve to guide me.
And when I'm grown I'll still reach out and know you're right beside me.

May the road rise to meet you

Traditional Irish blessing

May the road rise to meet you,
May the wind be always at your back.
May the sun shine warm upon your face,
The rains fall soft upon your fields.
And until we meet again,
May God hold you in the palm of his hand.

May God be with you and bless you;
May you see your children's children.
May you be poor in misfortune,
Rich in blessings,
May you know nothing but happiness
From this day forward.

May the road rise to meet you
May the wind be always at your back
May the warm rays of sun fall upon your home
And may the hand of a friend always be near.

May green be the grass you walk on,
May blue be the skies above you,
May pure be the joys that surround you,
May true be the hearts that love you.

If

Rudyard Kipling

If you can keep your head when all about you
Are losing theirs and blaming it on you,
If you can trust yourself when all men doubt you,
But make allowance for their doubting too;

If you can wait and not be tired by waiting,
Or being lied about, don't deal in lies,
Or being hated, don't give way to hating,
And yet don't look too good, nor talk too wise:

If you can dream – and not make dreams your master;
If you can think – and not make thoughts your aim;
If you can meet with Triumph and Disaster
And treat those two impostors just the same;

If you can bear to hear the truth you've spoken
Twisted by knaves to make a trap for fools,
Or watch the things you gave your life to, broken,
And stoop and build 'em up with worn-out tools:

If you can make one heap of all your winnings
And risk it on one turn of pitch-and-toss,
And lose, and start again at your beginnings
And never breathe a word about your loss;

If you can force your heart and nerve and sinew
To serve your turn long after they are gone,
And so hold on when there is nothing in you
Except the Will which says to them: 'Hold on!'

If you can talk with crowds and keep your virtue,
Or walk with Kings – nor lose the common touch,
If neither foes nor loving friends can hurt you,
If all men count with you, but none too much;

If you can fill the unforgiving minute
With sixty seconds' worth of distance run,
Yours is the Earth and everything that's in it,
And – which is more – you'll be a Man, my son!

A prayer for my daughter (extract)
W.B. Yeats

May she be granted beauty and yet not
Beauty to make a stranger's eye distraught,
Or hers before a looking-glass, for such,
Being made beautiful overmuch,
Consider beauty a sufficient end,
Lose natural kindness and maybe
The heart-revealing intimacy
That chooses right, and never find a friend.
May she become a flourishing, hidden tree,
That all her thoughts may like the linnet be,
And have no business but dispensing round
Their magnanimities of sound,
Nor but in merriment begin a chase,
Nor but in merriment a quarrel.
O may she live like some green laurel
Rooted in one dear perpetual place.

Poems for children to read

It's your birthday (extract)
John Maguire

This is the day you will never forget,
It's your red letter day;
We want to make it the happiest yet,
So we're coming to say.

We think it's great you're alive on this earth,
We celebrate your arrival at birth;
If you'll allow us, we'll join in your mirth,
It's your birthday, anything goes!
This is the day when you first took a bow,
The day you came onto the stage;
The show is still running and you're still a wow,
Baby you're all the rage!

No one can tell you just how it will go,
But we know well you're the star of the show,
Your life's the story let's start a new page,
It's your birthday, anything goes!

Us Two (extract from *Now We Are Six*)

A.A. Milne

Wherever I am, there's always Pooh,
There's always Pooh and Me.
Whatever I do, he wants to do,
'Where are you going today?' says Pooh.
'Well, that's very odd 'cos I was too'
'Let's go together,' says Pooh, says he.
'Let's go together,' says Pooh.

'What's twice eleven?' I said to Pooh.
('Twice what?' said Pooh to Me)
'I think it ought to be twenty-two.'
'Just what I think myself,' said Pooh.
'It wasn't an easy sum to do,
But that's what it is,' said Pooh, said he.
'That's what it is,' said Pooh.

'Let's look for dragons,' I said to Pooh.
'Yes, let's,' said Pooh to Me.
We crossed the river and found a few –
'Yes, those are dragons all right,' said Pooh.
'As soon as I saw their beaks I knew.
That's what they are,' said Pooh, said he.
'That's what they are,' said Pooh.
'Let's frighten the dragons,' I said to Pooh.
'That's right,' said Pooh to Me.
'I'm not afraid,' I said to Pooh,
And I held his paw and I shouted 'Shoo!
Silly old dragons!' – and off they flew.

'I wasn't afraid,' said Pooh, said he,
'I'm never afraid with you.'
So wherever I am, there's always Pooh,
There's always Pooh and Me.
'What would I do?' I said to Pooh,
'If it wasn't for you,' and Pooh said: 'True,
It isn't much fun for One, but Two,
Can stick together,' says Pooh, says he.
'That's how it is,' says Pooh.

Alice Through the Looking Glass (extract)
Lewis Carroll

Child of the pure unclouded brow
And dreaming eyes of wonder!
Though time be fleet, and I and thou
Are half a life asunder,
Thy loving smile will surely hail
The love-gift of a fairy-tale.

When I grow up
Avril Blight

I want to be a doctor,
And I want to be a nurse.
I'd like to be an artist,
Well, I'd like to write in verse.

I'm going to be a teacher.
I shall study law.
I'll navigate the sea in ships
With motor sails or oar.

Well, I shall be an engineer,
Make plans of roads and towns.
I'll be a circus performer
With other funny clowns.

You want to be an actor,
To sing and dance, be free,
But what I really want to do
Is simply to be me.

The Star
Jane Taylor

Twinkle, twinkle, little star,
How I wonder what you are!
Up above the world so high,
Like a diamond in the sky.
When the blazing sun is gone,
When he nothing shines upon,
Then you show your little light,
Twinkle, twinkle, all the night.
Then the traveller in the dark,
Thanks you for your tiny spark,
He could not see which way to go,
If you did not twinkle so.
In the dark blue sky you keep,

And often through my curtains peep,
For you never shut your eye,
Till the sun is in the sky.
As your bright and tiny spark,
Lights the traveller in the dark –
Though I know not what you are,
Twinkle, twinkle, little star.

Fairies

Rose Fyleman

There are fairies at the bottom of our garden!
It's not so very, very far away;
You pass the gardner's shed and you just keep straight ahead –
I do so hope they've really come to stay.
There's a little wood, with moss in it and beetles,
And a little stream that quietly runs through;
You wouldn't think they'd dare to come merrymaking there
Well, they do.

There are fairies at the bottom of our garden!
They often have a dance on summer nights;
The butterflies and bees make a lovely little breeze,
And the rabbits stand about and hold the lights.
Did you know that they could sit upon the moonbeams
And pick a little star to make a fan,
And dance away up there in the middle of the air   Well, they can.

There are fairies at the bottom of our garden!
You cannot think how beautiful they are;
They all stand up and sing when the Fairy Queen and King

Come gently floating down upon their car.
The King is very proud and very handsome;
The Queen – now you can guess who that could be
(She's a little girl all day, but at night she steals away) – Well – it's
Me!

Choosing a name (extract)
Mary Lamb

I have got a new-born sister.
I was the first one that kissed her.
She will shortly be to christen,
And papa has made the offer
I shall have the naming of her.

Now, I wonder what would please her –
Charlotte, Julia, or Louisa?
Ann and Mary, they're too common;
Joan's too formal for a woman;
Edith's pretty, but that looks
Better in old English books;
Ellen's left off long ago;
Blanche is out of fashion now.

None that I have named as yet
Are so good as Margaret.
Emily is neat and fine;
What do you think of Caroline?
How I'm puzzled and perplexed
What to choose or think of next!
I am in a little fever

Lest the name that I should give her
Should disgrace her or defame her: –
I will leave papa to name her.

---

case study

This is a lovely poem written by two big sisters for their baby sister. They have written a line for each letter in Beatrice's name, and this is an idea that an older sibling might like to try. It will certainly be unique, and will be loved by everyone listening.

Poem for Bea

Written by her older sisters, Elena and Ruby

B is for Beatrice, our little sister
E is for eating her dinner, messily
A is for A monkey
T is for the trampoline she likes to go on
R is for Ruby who likes playing with Bea
I is for I love my sister
C is for curly hair and crawling
E is for Elena, Ruby and Megan her big sisters

Poems with a religious theme

Above the bright blue sky
Albert Midlane

There's a Friend for little children
Above the bright blue sky,
A Friend who never changes
Whose love will never die;
Our earthly friends may fail us,
And change with changing years,
This Friend is always worthy
Of that dear name he bears.
There's a home for little children
Above the bright blue sky,
Where Jesus reigns in glory,
A home of peace and joy;
No home on earth is like it,
Nor can with it compare;
And everyone is happy,
Nor could be happier there.

And so the children come
Sophia Lyon Fahs

And so the children come.
And so they have been coming.
Always in the same way they come –
Born of the seed of man and woman.
No angels herald their beginning,

No prophets predict their future courses,
No wise men see a star to point their way
To find the babe that may save [hu]mankind.
Yet each night a child is born is a holy night.
Fathers and Mothers –
Sitting beside their children's cribs –
Feel glory in the wondrous sight of a life beginning.
They ask: 'When or how will this new life end?
Or will it ever end?'
Each night a child is born is a holy night.

Where did you come from?
George MacDonald (extract)

Where did you come from baby dear?
Out of the everywhere, into the here.
Where did you get your eyes so blue?
Out of the sky when I came through.
What makes your forehead so smooth and high?
A soft hand stroked it as I went by.
What makes your cheek like a warm, white rose?
Something better than anyone knows.
Where did you get that pearly ear?
God spoke, and it came out to hear.
How did they all just come to be you?
God thought about me and so I grew.
But how did you come to us Baby Dear?
God thought of you, and so I am here.

All things bright and beautiful
C.F. Alexander

All things bright and beautiful,
All creatures great and small,
All things wise and wonderful,
The Lord God made them all.

Each little flower that opens,
Each little bird that sings,
He made their glowing colours,
He made their tiny wings.

The purple-headed mountain,
The river running by,
The sunset and the morning,
That brightens up the sky;

The cold wind in the winter,
The pleasant summer sun,
The ripe fruits in the garden,
He made them every one;

The tall trees in the greenwood,
The meadows for our play,
The rushes by the water,
To gather every day;

He gave us eyes to see them,
And lips that we might tell
How great is God Almighty,
Who has made all things well.

Little things

Julia A. Carney

Little drops of water,
Little drains of sand,
Make the mighty ocean
And the beauteous land.
And the little moments,
Humble though they be,
Make the mighty ages
Of eternity.
So our little errors
Lead the soul away,
From the paths of virtue
Into sin to stray.
Little deeds of kindness,
Little words of love,
Make our earth an Eden,
Like the heaven above.

Readings

Many of the readings available for baby naming ceremonies are quite serious in nature, but a well-chosen extract may add a little gravitas to the occasion, particularly if read by an older member of the family. Do feel free to choose only a small part of a reading. It is good idea to practise reading these out loud, so you can time the reading and work out how best to deliver it without becoming too serious.

Meditation on the upbringing of children
Dorothy Louise-Law Nolte

If a child lives with criticism
he learns to condemn.
If a child lives with hostility
he learns to fight.
If a child lives with ridicule
he learns to be shy.
If a child lives with shame
he learns to feel guilt.

But, If a child lives with tolerance
he learns to be patient.
If a child lives with encouragement
he learns confidence.
If a child lives with fairness
he learns justice.
If a child lives with security
he learns to have faith.

If a child lives with approval
he learns to like himself.
If a child lives with acceptance and friendship
he learns to find love in the world.

(*Children Learn from What They Live: Parenting to Inspire Values*,
Workman Publishing, 1998.)

May all your wishes come true
Unknown author

May all your wishes come true.
May you always do for others, and let others do for you.
May you build a ladder to the stars and climb on every rung,
And may you stay forever young.
May you grow to be righteous,
May you grow up to be true,
May you always know the truth, and see the light that's
surrounding you.

May you always be courageous, stand upright and be strong,
And may you stay forever young.
May your hands always be busy, and may your feet always be
swift.
May you have a strong foundation when the winds of change
shift.
May your heart always be joyful, and may your song always be
sung,
And may you stay forever young.

The Prophet (extract)
Kahlil Gibran

And a woman who held a babe against her bosom said, speak to
us of Children. And he said:

Your children are not your children.
They are the sons and daughters
of Life's longing for itself.

They come through you but not from you.
And though they are with you
yet they belong not to you.

You may give them your love
but not your thoughts,
For they have their own thoughts,
You may house their bodies
but not their souls
For their souls dwell in the house of tomorrow,
which you cannot visit
not even in your dreams.

You may strive to be like them,
but seek not to make them like you,
For life goes not backward
nor tarries with yesterday.
You are simply the bows from which your children
as living arrows are sent forth.

(Pan Books, 1923.)

A child is the only point
Maria Montessori

A child is the only point on which there converges from everyone a feeling of love and gentleness. People's souls soften and sweeten when one speaks of children. The whole of mankind shares in the deep emotions which they awaken. The child is a well-spring of love.

Desiderata
Max Ehrmann

Go placidly amid the noise and haste,
And remember what peace there may be in silence.
As far as possible without surrender,
Be on good terms with all persons.
Speak your truth quietly and clearly:
And listen to others,
Even the dull and ignorant:
They too have their story.

Avoid loud and aggressive persons,
They are vexations to the spirit.
If you compare yourself with others,
You may become vain and bitter:
For always there will be greater and lesser persons than yourself.
Enjoy your achievements as well as your plans.

Keep interested in your own career, however humble:
It is a real possession in the changing fortunes of time.

Exercise caution in business affairs:
For the world is full of trickery.
But let this not blind you to what virtue there is:
Many persons strive for high ideals:
And everywhere life is full of heroism.

Be yourself.
Especially, do not feign affection.
Neither be cynical about love:
For in the face of all aridity and disenchantment,
It is as perennial as the grass.

Take kindly the counsel of the years,
Gracefully surrendering the things of youth.
Nurture strength of spirit to shield you in sudden misfortune.
But do not distress yourself with dark imaginings.
Many fears are born of fatigue and loneliness.
Beyond a wholesome discipline,
Be gentle with yourself.

You are a child of the universe,
No less than the trees and the stars.
You have a right to be here.
And whether or not it is clear to you,
No doubt the universe is unfolding as it should.

Therefore be at peace with God,
Whatever you conceive him to be.
And whatever your labours and aspirations,
In the noisy confusion of life keep peace with your soul.

With all its sham and drudgery, and broken dreams,
It is a beautiful world.
Be cheerful.
Strive to be happy.

(Hard Press)

Look to this day
Sanskrit text

Look to this day … for it is the very life of life:
In its brief course lie all the realities and truths of existence.
The joy of growth, the splendour of action, the glory of power.
For yesterday is but a memory and tomorrow is only a vision …
But today – well lived – makes eery yesterday
A memory of happiness,
And every tomorrow a vision of hope.
Look well therefore to this day.

This World, My Home (extract)
Kenneth L. Patton

Nothing is strange to the child for whom everything is new.
Where all things are new nothing is novel.
The child does not yet know what belongs and what does not;
    therefore for him all things belong.
The ear of the child is open to all music.
The eyes are open to all arts.
His mind is open to all tongues.
His being is open to all manners.
In the child's country there are no foreigners.

Lessons for Children to Learn

Unknown author

Do not be bored with childhood so that you rush to grow up –
and then long to be a child again.

Do not lose your health to make money – you'll lose your money
to restore your health.

Do not think so anxiously about the future that you forget the
present and end up living neither.

Do not live as though you will never die, or you will die as
though you have never lived.

Learn that you cannot make someone love you, all you can do is
let yourself be loved.

Learn that it is neither interesting nor helpful to compare
yourself with others.

Learn to forgive by practising forgiveness.

Learn that it only takes a few seconds to open profound wounds
in those whom we love and it can take many years to heal
them.

Learn that there will be those that love you dearly but who have
not learned how to express or show their feelings.

Learn that two people can look at the same thing and see it
entirely differently.

Learn that a rich person is not the one who has the most, but the
one who needs the least to be happy.

Learn that it is not enough for you to forgive others, you must
also forgive yourself.

May you live to love, and may you love, always
Unknown author

We wish you long life and much happiness.
May you face all challenges that come to you as a person of integrity,
May you continue to bring great joy to your parents, your
grandparents, family, friends, and to all those who come to know
   you.
May beauty delight you and happiness uplift you,
May wonder fulfill you and love surround you.
May your step be steady and your arm be strong,
May your heart be peaceful and your word be true.
May you seek to learn, may you learn to live.
May you live to love, and may you love, always.

The role of a parent (extract)
Brock Chisholm

It is becoming generally recognised that the role of the parent
in relation to the upbringing of a child is perhaps the most
important thing that happens in our culture. Our responsibility
is to help children learn things and learn in ways that were not
available to us when we were children. If they are going to make
the kind of world in which security can be found, they will have
to develop free of many limitations that still bind us.

Many people who themselves have developed away from 'certainties',
religious or otherwise, inculcated in them in their childhood, send
their children back, by their own teaching or by that of others, to
learn things in terms which they themselves have discarded.
This is unfair to children. Surely one's children should be given

the advantage of one's own development. Surely they should not be tied hand and foot all over again as their parents were tied to the absolutes of the past generation. Each generation should let its children continue from the point it itself has reached.

(*Can people learn to learn?* George Allen and Unwin, 1958.)

Let our children learn to be honest (extract)
A. Powell Davies

Let our children learn to be honest, both with themselves and with others. Honesty is the ability to distinguish between what is and what is not, and thus to deal effectively with reality.

Let our children learn to love truth. When truth is present, there is no prejudice. By fidelity to truth the mind is nourished.

Let our children discover their strengths and find courage.

Let our children cultivate kindness, tolerance and acceptance of other people. These abilities do not come without cultivation.

Let our children learn that they are like others, even people they do not like; and that there is good and bad in all of us.

Tao Te Ching (extract)

Giving birth and nourishing,
having without possessing,
acting with no expectations,
leading and not trying to control:
this is the supreme virtue.

The firstborn (extract)
Laurie Lee

What have I got exactly? And what am I going to do with her?
And what, for that matter, will she do with me?

I have got a daughter, whose life is already separate from mine,
whose will already follows its own directions, and who has
quickly corrected my woolly preconceptions of her by being
remorselessly different. She is the child of herself and will be
what she is. I am merely the keep of her temporary helplessness.

At this stage in my life she will give me more than she gets,
and may even later become my keeper. But if I could teach her
anything at all, by unloading upon her some of the ill-tied parcels
of my years, I'd like it to be acceptance and a relish for life.

(*Poems and Readings for Christenings*, ed. Susannah Steel, New
Holland Publishers, 2009.)

Know you what it is to be a child?

Francis Thompson

Know you what it is to be a child? It is to be something very
different from the man of today.
It is to have a spirit yet streaming from the waters of baptism;
It is to believe in love, to believe in loveliness, to believe in belief;
It is to be so little that the elves can reach to whisper in your ear;
It is to turn pumpkins into coaches, and mice into horses,
lowness into loftiness, and nothing into everything, for each child
has a fairy godmother in his/her own soul;
It is to live in a nutshell and count yourself the king/queen of
infinite space;
It is: To see the world in a grain of sand, And a heaven in a wild
flower,
Hold infinity in the palm of your hand, And eternity in an hour.

Give us the spirit of the child

Unknown author

Give us the child who lives within – the child who trusts, the
child who imagines, the child who sings, the child who receives
without reservation, the child who gives without judgement.

Give us a child's eyes, that we may receive the beauty and
freshness of this day like a sunrise.

Give us a child's ears, that we may hear the music of mythical times.

Give us a child's heart, that we may be filled with wonder and
delight.

Give us a child's faith, that we may be cured of our cynicism.

Give us the spirit of the child, who is not afraid to need, who is not afraid to love.

Declaration of the Rights of the Child
United Nations, General Assembly, 1959

Children have rights:

The right to equality, regardless of race, colour, religion, sex and nationality

The right to healthy mental and physical development

The right to a name and nationality

The right to sufficient food, housing and medical care

The right to special care if handicapped

The right to love, understanding and care

The right to free education, play and recreation

The right to immediate aid in the event of disasters and emergencies

The right to protection from cruelty, neglect, and exploitation.

The right to protection from persecution and to an upbringing in the spirit of [sisterhood], brotherhood and peace.

Other poems and readings you might like to consider

29 April 1989 by Sujata Bhatt published by Carcanet

The Gift by Rabindranath Tagore from *Selected Poems*, Penguin Classics, 2005

On the Seashore by Rabindranath Tagore from *Selected Poems*, Penguin Classics, 2005

You're by Sylvia Plath from *Ariel*, Faber and Faber, included in various editions and anthologies.

Born Yesterday by Philip Larkin from *Collected Poems*, Faber and Faber, 2003.

I'd love to be a fairy's child by Robert Graves from *The Complete Poems*, Penguin Modern Classics, 2003.

Ode on the whole duty of parents by Frances Cornford from *Selected Poems*, Enitharmon Press, 1996.

Choosing a name by Anne Ridler, from *Collected Poems*, Carcanet Press, 1997.

From a matter of life and death by Anne Ridler, from *Collected Poems*, Carcanet Press, 1997.

Song for a young mother by Edith Joy Scovell from *Women's Poetry of the 1930s*, Routledge, 1995.

There is a song in man by Spike Milligan, Virgin Books

Extract from **The Tao of Pooh** by Benjamin Hoff – first lines:

'You can be a guiding star
If you make the most of who you are'

CHAPTER SIX

Choosing a name for your baby

Wow, what a difficult choice! There are so many reasons for choosing a particular name for your child, it can be difficult to decide on just one. You may opt for a traditional route and choose a family name that has been used for generations, or you may choose something you simply love the sound of. The name of a favourite writer, artist or musician may appeal, as it has positive associations for you, or you may want to choose something unusual to make sure your child is the only one with his or her name in their class.

To help you, here is the most recent list based on UK government statistics of names that are the most popular at the moment. Statistics have shown that names can vary in popularity from region to region, so you may choose a name that is in the top ten list, but find that very few of your neighbours have chosen it.

The meaning of names can be hard to pin down. You can trace the first use of a name or the Old English and Biblical origins, but this can sometimes only give you clues as to why it is now popular or well-liked. The best course of action is to choose a name that you both really like, rather than try to second-guess what is popular or trendy as it changes so often.

Most popular boys' names in England and Wales

❶ Jack
❷ Oliver
❸ Thomas
❹ Harry
❺ Joshua
❻ Alfie
❼ Charlie
❽ Daniel
❾ James
❿ William

Most popular girls' names in England and Wales

❶ Olivia
❷ Ruby
❸ Emily
❹ Grace
❺ Jessica
❻ Chloe
❼ Sophie
❽ Lily
❾ Amelia
❿ Evie

(From Office for National Statistics, 2008. Last updated September 2009.)

Appendix

Further reading and resources

Register Offices

www.direct.gov.uk
Information on finding your local register office and the law for registering your baby.

Goddess naming ceremonies

Priestess of Avalon, Priestess of the Goddess by Kathy Jones
Arianne publication
www.kathyjones.co.uk

Humanist naming ceremonies

New Arrivals by Jane Wynne Willson and Robert Ashby
British Humanist Association

Civil ceremonies

Your Complete Guide to Naming Ceremonies by Anne Barber
GA Publishing

Civil Naming Ceremonies

www.civilceremonies.co.uk

The Balloon Association

www.nabas.co.uk
Guidelines for balloon release.

The Poetry Archive

www.poetryarchive.org
Resource for poetry.

The Woodland Trust

www.woodlandtrust.org.uk
Guidelines and schemes for planting trees.

Sponsoring a child

www.worldvision.org.uk
www.actionaid.org.uk
www.children.org
Organisations that help you to sponsor a child.

Naming a star

www.starlistings.co.uk
www.starregistery.co.uk
Just two of the companies who offer star naming.

Owning a piece of the moon

www.moonestates.com

Adopting an animal

www.wwf-adopt-an-animal.org.uk
www.ethicalgifts.co.uk
www.bornfree.org.uk
www.farmanimalrescue.org.uk
www.bluecross.org.uk
Organisations that help you to sponsor or adopt an animal.

Naming a rose/finding a rose

www.countrygardenroses.co.uk
Just one site who can advise on purchasing roses.

Thanks to...

I'd like to thank the families who shared their experiences and ideas with me, especially Tina, Kavida, Helen, Ruth, Ceri and Becca. Also thanks to Elena and Ruby for their lovely poem. Thanks also to Izzie, Polly and Steve for inspiring me to write this book for all the families out there who would like to do something a little different.

Also thanks to Nikki Read for the go-ahead and Rebecca and Michelle for their fresh eyes.

Some other titles from How To Books

Cooking With Mrs Simkins
How to cook simple, wholesome, home-made meals

In this book you'll find good wholesome recipes that you can make yourself whatever your level of expertise.

For the novice cook it offers step by step guidance and encouragement by explaining the recipes in a straightforward and accessible way. For the more experienced cook it offers new recipes and fresh ways of doing things.

Mrs Simkins understands the importance of good home cooking. In this book she shares some of the delicious but economical recipes that she has cooked over the years for her own family and friends:

- hearty hot dinners and roasts
- light lunches
- simple soothing soups
- plenty of baking (including pastry and sponge cakes)
- perfect puddings
- tempting toasty snacks
- plus how to make your own bread with a bread maker.

A regular columnist for the well-loved Blackmore Vale Magazine in the West Country, Mrs Simkins writes with the benefit of a lifetime of cooking for her friends and family and children.

ISBN   978-1-905862-36-8

Eat Well, Spend Less
Sarah Flower

A leading nutritionist and journalist, and author of *Live More, Spend Less*, Sarah has put together a treasure trove of quick, easy and affordable recipes which are also designed to maintain and enhance your health. Her easy-to-use meal planner will literally transform the lives of busy families.

The delicious, easy-to-follow and wholesome recipes in this book cost as little as 25p a portion.

- Store cupboard know-how and storage facts
- Cooking guidelines for maximum healthiness and nutrition
- Fast food that's actually good for you
- Super soups
- Magnificent meaty meals
- Fabulous fishy fare
- Various veggie victuals
- Sumptuous salads
- Desserts, cakes, and snack attacks
- Menu planning to improve wellbeing

Sarah Flower is a nutritionist, a magazine columnist, and author of *Live More, Spend Less, Slow Cook, Fast Food* and *Eat Well, Spend Less*. She is a mother of two and lives with her family in North Devon.

ISBN   978-1-905862-39-9

Slow Cook, Fast Food
*Over 250 healthy, wholesome slow cooker
and one pot meals for all the family*

Sarah Flower

In this book nutritionist Sarah Flower offers advice for the busy family to literally take things *slowly*. Slow cooking is the easiest way to cook, plus it has the added advantage of being good for your health. And you don't have to slave over a hot stove when you've finished work for the day to create your supper. Literally fill your slow cooker with your chosen ingredients and walk away for the day. Nothing could be simpler.

Slow Cook, Fast Food also shows you how to save on washing up by creating one pot meals and desserts for all the family without breaking a sweat.

- Use your slow cooker to make nutritious meals with very little effort
- Prepare one pot dishes with ease – and less washing up!
- Prepare mouth watering soups, main meals and desserts
- Make the most of your ingredients with helpful store cupboard tips
- Discover great tips and advice for saving time and money

ISBN   978-1-905862-41-2

How To Grow Great Kids
The good parents' guide to rearing sociable, confident and healthy children
Allison Lee

This invaluable guide for parents is divided into two parts. Part One will help you to: encourage your child's social and self-help skills; manage your child's behaviour successfully; and promote your child's emotional wellbeing.

Part Two starts with the stages of development from birth through to adolescence and shows you how to produce healthy balanced meals; and minimise the risks of allergies and intolerances.

ISBN   978-1-84528-288-2

The Working Mum's Guide To Childcare
How to choose and manage the right childcare for your child
Allison Lee

'If you are fortunate to have a choice, this'll help you make the right one.'
Families South East

This book looks at the most popular types of childcare available and weighs up the advantages and disadvantages of each to help you to decide which service suits you best. It will help you to decide what kind of childcare you require; ensure that the relationship between the child and the carer and you and the carer work well; know what to expect from your childminder in terms of play and educational activities; know what to do when either your child or the carer is ill; understand the childcare contract and know what to do when things go wrong.

ISBN   978-1-84528-378-0

How To Books are available through all good bookshops, or you can order direct from us through Grantham Book Services.

Tel: +44 (0)1476 541080
Fax: +44 (0)1476 541061
Email: orders@gbs.tbs-ltd.co.uk

Or via our website
www.howtobooks.co.uk

To order via any of these methods please quote the title(s) of the book(s) and your credit card number together with its expiry date.

For further information about our books and catalogue, please contact:

How To Books
Spring Hill House
Spring Hill Road
Begbroke
Oxford
OX5 1RX

Visit our website at
www.howtobooks.co.uk

Or you can contact us by email at info@howtobooks.co.uk